Gardiner on Cromwell

"OLIVER'S CLAIM to greatness can be tested by the undoubted fact that his character receives higher and wider appreciation as the centuries pass by. The limitations on his nature—the one-sidedness of his religious zeal, the mistakes of his policy—are thrust out of sight; the nobility of his motives, the strength of his character, and the breadth of his intellect force themselves on the minds of generations for which the objects for which he strove have been for the most part attained, though often in a different fashion from that which he placed before himself. Even those who refuse to waste a thought on his spiritual aims remember with gratitude his constancy of effort to make England great by land and sea; and it would be well for them also to be reminded of his no less constant efforts to make England worthy of greatness."

SAMUEL RAWSON GARDINER

OLIVER

CROMWELL

With a New Introduction by

MAURICE ASHLEY

COLLIER BOOKS
NEW YORK, N.Y.

Collier Books is a division of The Crowell-Collier Publishing Company

First Collier Books Edition 1962

Library of Congress Catalog Card Number: 62-12074

Hecho en los E.E.U.U.
Printed in the United States of America

Introduction

Introduction

SOON AFTER Samuel Rawson Gardiner's death on February 23, 1902, the famous American historian, James Ford Rhodes, went so far as to compare him with Charles Darwin as "almost the only perfectly disinterested lover of truth." Another American historian, Edward Channing, said: "I firmly believe that Mr. Gardiner is the greatest historical writer who has appeared since Gibbon."

Gardiner, who was born on March 4, 1829, dedicated practically the whole of his working life to pioneering research into the history of Great Britain in the seventeenth century. Although he took a first-class degree at Oxford University and was awarded a Studentship (or Fellowship) at Christ Church, he was not able to pursue his chosen work there on account of his unusual religion. For he had become a member of the Catholic Apostolic Church, founded by Edward Irving, whose youngest daughter he married in 1855. They settled in London and he had to depend largely on teaching or writing textbooks for his living (before he died he was twice married and left eight children); he gave instruction in private schools and lectured at London University; in 1877 he was appointed Professor of Modern History at King's College. But on many days every year he was to be found in the British Museum laboring on his projected masterpiece, a history of England from the accession of King James I to the death of Oliver Cromwell.

This was the work that gained Gardiner his world reputation. Before it neared completion he was given a Civil List pension by the British Prime Minister, Mr. Gladstone; he was elected to two research Fellowships at Oxford; and he was even offered the academic accolade, the Regius Professorship of Modern History at Oxford, which he refused, as it would have meant too much time away from his beloved labors in the British Museum.

Gardiner's method of writing history was as follows: first, he would attempt to read everything that was available about his subject in every language (he could read most European languages) whether in print or in manuscript; having digested that, he would endeavor to shut his mind to any knowledge he possessed except about the period on which he was then engaged; he believed passionately in a strict adherence to chronology. "If he was working at the year 1653 he would decline material relating to 1654. 'I am not ready for that yet,' he would say in his inexpressibly gentle way." He usually wrote in the British Museum in the midst of all his manuscripts and pamphlets. He wrote rapidly, corrected little, and after a few pages were finished he would send them off directly to the printer. Though he kept in touch with everything that was written or discovered about his subject and admitted that he was liable to error, when revising his book he was more concerned about rearranging his presentation than over altering his arguments. In substance most of what he wrote remains as valid today as when it was written in the mid-Victorian period; and the facts that he unearthed have been absorbed into the body of historical knowledge.

Two volumes of his history were published at a time. When the first two appeared they were somewhat critically received and a mere hundred or so copies were sold. Gradually, however, the assiduity and single-mindedness of his toil came to be generally appreciated: "We know the history of England from 1603 to 1656 better than we do that of any other period of the world," asserted J. F. Rhodes in 1902, "and for this we are indebted mainly to Samuel Rawson Gardiner." Academic honors and praises were showered upon him everywhere. His eighteen volumes were acclaimed by his pupil, Sir Charles Firth, as "an achievement of permanent value." Though Gardiner did not live to complete his main work down to the death of Oliver Cromwell (Firth himself did this), he left in his lectures entitled *Cromwell's Place* (1897) and in his book on Oliver Cromwell, written for Goupil's series of illustrated biographies in 1899, epitomes of his own views on the celebrated Puritan English statesman, from whom, curiously enough, he himself was directly descended.

Gardiner's *Oliver Cromwell* was first published exactly three hundred years after Cromwell's birth and contains the mature reflections of one of the most learned of all students of seventeenth-century British history. That is why it is worth reading again now. Though he recognized that Cromwell had his faults, Gardiner admired him profoundly. He said of his hero: "He stands forth as the typical Englishman of the modern world. . . . It is time for us to regard him as he really was, with all his physical and moral audacity, with all his tenderness and spiritual yearnings, in the world of action what Shakespeare was in the world of thought, the greatest because the most typical Englishman of all time."

"The typical Englishman of the modern world." Gardiner was of course thinking of the world in which he himself had grown up, a world where Puritanism was rife, where the ruling classes were still much the same as they had been since the Protestant Reformation, where the middle classes were enjoying a Golden Age, where the hard-working mechanic was idolized, where education was highly respected, where people read the Bible voraciously, where Britain was still perhaps the greatest power and empire upon earth. In Gardiner's book on Cromwell we are gazing at the Puritan hero through mid-Victorian eyes. It is true that since the middle of the nineteenth century "scientific history" (which one associates particularly with the name of Leopold von Ranke, also a student of the seventeenth century) had become more and more fashionable. Yet when Gardiner's books were first published they were damply received, partly because he did not write in the same vivacious style as Gibbon, Macaulay, or Froude. But this very pedestrian character of his writing in time earned him confidence and respect. Gardiner did not believe in fancy writing; and it is said that it was only when he learned about the magnificent illustrations and letterpress that

Goupil intended to provide for his life of Cromwell that he felt "obliged to try after a better style than he usually wrote."

The other criticism that has generally been made of Gardiner is that he placed too much importance on his chronological method. In defending him, Firth asked whether there is in fact any better method of writing history. Be that as it may, it clearly has its disadvantages if too rigorously pursued. And the American historian, Roland G. Usher, in his book on *The Historical Method of Samuel Rawson Gardiner*, published in 1915 has, to my mind at least, conclusively exposed the weaknesses of his method. Gardiner's ideas about the English nation, the English constitution, and even some of the characters in his history are inconsistent and not always convincing. The truth is that it is not enough to be wedded to one's seat in the British Museum, and, as I have argued elsewhere,* historians less learned than Gardiner but understanding more about political life, such as Guizot and Theodore Roosevelt, were better schooled to grasp a statesman's problems.

In the United States today (though less so in Britain) there has been some reaction against the idea of history as a science in the sense that the pupils of Von Ranke and Gardiner believed it to be. Few people now would seriously compare the study of history with the method of the physical sciences. Even if precise agreement could be reached upon the "facts" of history, their presentation requires the work of an artist, which is not always forthcoming and is sometimes even despised in university circles. The very focus brought to bear on these historical facts varies from generation to generation and sometimes distorts them; and our focus in the Nuclear Age is very different from that of the relatively self-assured times in which Gardiner worked.

Even the facts themselves may have an elusive quality. For example, in the first chapter of his *Oliver Cromwell* Gardiner refers to Thomas Cromwell as a "despotic" Minister; that view is no longer generally accepted. Gardiner bases his belief that Oliver's father was "a man of sober Puritanism" on a portrait of him that is no longer believed to be genuine, while the por-

* *The Greatness of Oliver Cromwell.*

trait of Oliver to which he refers in Sidney Sussex College, Cambridge, is now thought to be an indifferent eighteenth-century copy. Gardiner also had the habit of relying upon stories or anecdotes whose provenance was doubtful, if they fitted in with his own preconceived notion of Oliver Cromwell's character. There are three instances in this book. Though he admits that entries about Cromwell's public penitences in the parish register of St. John's church in Huntingdon are forgeries, Gardiner suggests that the forger may have had "a recollection that something of the kind had happened within local memory." An anecdote, dating from after Cromwell's death, about how a letter from King Charles I written to his Queen was intercepted at the Blue Boar inn in Holborn by Cromwell and his son-in-law disguised as common troopers is used to illustrate Cromwell's changed belief about the King's trustworthiness. And an even more improbable story about Cromwell gazing at the King's decapitated body after his execution and sighing "Cruel necessity!" is said by Gardiner to have "much to recommend it." All this merely goes to show that every writer on his history, however scientific he aims to be, employs his own imagination to interpret character and is tempted to select the evidence to suit his own line of argument.

But whatever defects may be detected in Gardiner's style, approach, or historical method, those of us who have written on seventeenth-century history owe an immense debt to Gardiner and indeed could not have produced our own books without drawing upon his vast accumulation of material and acknowledging our gratitude to his selfless devotion to his subject. Every generation must interpret the character of Oliver Cromwell for itself and—to be perfectly honest—I doubt if any generation except his own has ever understood him. But in any case he is an outstanding figure in the history of the world as a statesman, a soldier, and a Christian. Few historians will agree about his character or achievement, though the more they know, the less dogmatic they become. He was certainly no chemical compound capable of analysis upon a laboratory table. We cannot read about him too often.

October, 1961 MAURICE ASHLEY

Table of Contents

Oliver Cromwell

Chapter 1

King and Parliament

OLIVER CROMWELL, the future Lord Protector of the Commonwealth of England, was born at Huntingdon on April 25, 1599, receiving his baptismal name from his uncle, Sir Oliver Cromwell of Hinchingbrooke, a mansion hard by the little town. It was at Huntingdon that the father of the infant, Robert Cromwell, had established himself, farming lands and perhaps also adding to his income by the profits of a brewhouse managed by his wife, Elizabeth—a descendant of a middle-class Norfolk family of Steward—originally Styward—which, whatever writers of authority may say, was not in any way connected with the Royal House of Scotland.

"I was," said Cromwell in one of his later speeches, "by birth a gentleman, living neither in any considerable height nor yet in obscurity. I have been called to several employments in the nation, and—not to be overtedious—I did endeavour to discharge the duty of an honest man in those services to God and His people's interest, and to the Commonwealth." The open secret of Cromwell's public life is set forth in these words—his aim being: first, to be himself an honest man; secondly, to serve God and the people of God; and thirdly, to fulfil his duty to the Commonwealth. In this order, and in no other, did his obligations to his fellow-creatures present themselves to his eyes. For the work before him it could not be otherwise than helpful that his position in life brought him into contact with all classes of society.

What powers and capacities this infant—or indeed any other infant—may have derived from this or the other ancestor, is a mystery too deep for human knowledge; but at least it may be noted that the descent of the Cromwells from Sir Richard Williams, the nephew of Thomas Cromwell, the despotic Minister of Henry VIII, brought into the family a Welsh strain which may have shown itself in the fervid idealism lighting up the stern practical sense of the warrior and statesman.

Of Oliver's father little is known; but his portrait testifies that he was a man of sober Puritanism, not much given to any form of spiritual enthusiasm—very unlike his elder brother, Sir Oliver, who had inherited not only the estate, but the splendid ways of his father, Sir Henry Cromwell—the Golden Knight—and who, after running through his property, was compelled to sell his land and to retire into a more obscure position. As the little Oliver grew up, he had before his eyes the types of the future Cavalier and Roundhead in his own family. So far as parental influence could decide the question, there could be no doubt on which side the young Oliver would take his stand. His education was carried on in the free school of the town, under Dr. Beard, the author of *The Theatre of God's Judgments Displayed*, in which a belief in the constant intervention of Providence in the punishment of offenders was set forth by numerous examples of the calamities of the wicked. Though Oliver afterwards learned to modify the crudeness of this teaching, the doctrine that success or failure was an indication of Divine favour or disfavour never left him, and he was able, in the days of his greatness, to point unhesitatingly to the results of Naseby and Worcester as evidence that God Himself approved of the victorious cause.

In 1616 Cromwell matriculated at Sidney Sussex College, Cambridge, where his portrait now adorns the walls of the

College hall. After a sojourn of no more than a year, he left the University, probably—as his father died in that year—to care for his widowed mother and his five sisters, he himself being now the only surviving son. It is said that not long afterwards he settled in London to study law, and though there is no adequate authority for this statement, it derives support from the fact that he found a wife in London, marrying in 1620, at the early age of twenty-one, Elizabeth Bourchier, the daughter of a City merchant. The silence of contemporaries shows that, in an age when many women took an active part in politics, she confined herself to the sphere of domestic influence. The one letter of hers that is preserved displays not merely her affectionate disposition, but also her helpfulness in reminding her great husband of the necessity of performing those little acts of courtesy which men engaged in large affairs are sometimes prone to neglect. She was undoubtedly a model of female perfection after the Periclean standard.

Of Cromwell's early life for some years after his marriage we have little positive information. His public career was opened by his election in 1628 to sit for Huntingdon in the Parliament which insisted on the Petition of Right. Though his uncle had by this time left Hinchingbrooke, and could therefore have had no direct influence on the electors, it is quite likely that the choice of his fellow-townsmen was, to a great extent, influenced by their desire to show their attachment to a family with which they had long been in friendly relation.

Even so, however, it is in the highest degree improbable that Cromwell would have been selected by his neighbours, to whom every action of his life had been laid open, unless they had had reason to confide in his moral worth as well as in his aptitude for public business. Yet it is in this period of his life that, if Royalist pamphleteers are to be credited, Cromwell was wallowing in revolting profligacy, and the charge may seem to find some support from his own language in a subsequent letter to his cousin, Mrs. St. John: "You know," he wrote, "what my manner of life hath been. Oh! I lived in and loved darkness, and hated light. I was a chief—the chief of sinners. This is true, I hated godliness, yet God had mercy upon me." It has however never been wise to take the expressions of a converted penitent literally, and it is enough to suppose that Cromwell had been, at least whilst an undergraduate at Cambridge, a buoyant, unthinking youth, fond of outdoor exercise; though, on the other hand, whilst he never attained to proficiency as a scholar, he by no means neglected the authorised studies of the place. Much as opinion has differed on every other point in his character, there was never any doubt as to his love of horses and to his desire to encourage men of learning. It may fairly be argued that his tastes in either direction must have been acquired in youth.

One piece of evidence has indeed been put forward against Cromwell. On the register of St. John's parish at Huntingdon are two entries—one dated 1621, and the other 1628—stating that Cromwell submitted in those years to some form of Church censure. The formation of the letters, however, the absence of any date of month or day, and also the state of the parchment on which the entries occur, leave no reasonable doubt that they were the work of a forger. It does not follow that the forger had not a recollection that something of the kind had happened within local memory, and if we take it as possible that Cromwell was censured for "his deeds," whatever they may have been, in 1621, and that in 1628 he voluntarily acknowledged some offence—the wording of the forged entry gives some countenance to this deduction—may we not note a coincidence of date between the second entry and one in the diary of Sir Theodore Mayerne—the fashionable physician of the day—who notes that Oliver Cromwell, who visited him in September of that year, was *valde melancholicus*. Even if no heed whatever is to be paid to the St. John's register, Mayerne's statement enables us approximately to date that time of mental struggle which he passed through at some time in these years, and which was at last brought to an end when the contemplation of his own unworthiness yielded to the assurance of his Saviour's love. "Whoever yet," he wrote long afterwards to his daughter Bridget, "tasted that the Lord is gracious, without some sense of self, vanity and badness?" It was a crisis in his life which, if he had been born in the Roman communion, would probably have sent him—as it sent Luther—into a monastery. Being what he was, a Puritan Englishman, it left him with strong resolution to do his work in this world strenuously, and to help others in things temporal, as he himself had been helped in things spiritual.

English Puritanism, like other widely spread influences, was complex in its nature, leading to different results in different men. Intellectually it was based on the Calvinistic theology, and many were led on by it to the fiercest intolerance of all systems of thought and practice which were unconformable thereto. Cromwell's nature was too large, and his character too strong, to allow him long to associate himself with the bigots of his age. His Puritanism—if not as universally sympathetic as a modern philosopher might wish—was moral rather than intellectual. No doubt it rendered him impatient of the outward forms in which the religious devotion of such contemporaries as George Herbert and Crashaw found appropriate sustenance, but at the same time it held him back from bowing down to the idol of the men of his own party—the requirement of accurate conformity to the Calvinistic standard of belief. It was sufficient for him, if he and his associates found inspiration in a sense of personal dependence on God, issuing forth in good and beneficent deeds.

When, in 1628, Cromwell took his seat in the House of Commons he would be sure of a good reception as a cousin of Hampden. There is, however, nothing to surprise us in his silence during the eventful debates on the Petition of Right. He was no orator by nature, though he could express himself forcibly when he felt deeply, and at this time, and indeed during the whole of his life, he felt more deeply on religious than on political questions. The House, in its second session held in 1629, was occupied during the greater portion of its time with religious questions, and it was then that Cromwell made his first speech, if so short an utterance can be dignified by that name. "Dr. Beard," he informed the House, "told him that one Dr. Alablaster did at the Spital preach in a sermon tenets of Popery, and Beard being to repeat the same, the now Bishop of Winton, then Bishop of Lincoln, did send for Dr. Beard, and charged him as his diocesan, not to preach any doctrine contrary to that which Alablaster had delivered, and when Beard did, by the advice of Bishop Felton, preach against Dr. Alablaster's sermon and person, Dr. Neile, now Bishop of Winton, did reprehend him, the said Beard, for it."

The circumstances of the time give special biographical importance to the opening of this window into Cromwell's mind. The strife between the Puritan clergy and the Court prelates was waxing high. The latter, whilst anxious to enforce discipline, and the external usages which, though enjoined in the Prayer Book, had been neglected in many parts of the country, were at the same time contending for a broader religious teaching than that presented by Calvin's logic; but knowing that they were in a comparatively small minority they, perhaps not unnaturally, fell back on the protection of the King, who was in ecclesiastical matters completely under the influence of Laud. The result of Charles's consultations with such Bishops as were at hand had been the issue of a Declaration which was prefixed to a new edition of the articles, and is to be found in Prayer Books at the present day. The King's remedy for disputes in the Church on predestination and such matters was to impose silence on both parties, and it was in view of this policy that Cromwell raked up an old story to show how at least twelve years before, his old schoolmaster, Dr. Beard, had been forbidden to preach any doctrine but that which the member for Huntingdon stigmatised as Popish, and this too by a prelate who was now seeking, in a less direct way, to impose silence on Puritan ministers. Other members of Parliament had striven to oppose the ecclesiasticism of the Court by the intolerant assertion that Calvinism alone was to be preached. Cromwell did nothing of the kind. He did not even say that those who upheld what he calls "tenets of Popery" were to be silenced. He merely asked that those who objected to them might be free to deliver their testimony in public. There is the germ here of his future liberal policy as Lord Protector—the germ too of a wide difference of opinion from those with whom he was at this time acting in concert.*

Little as we know of Cromwell's proceedings during the eleven years in which no Parliament sat, that little is significant. His interference in temporal affairs was invariably on the side of the poor. In 1630 a new charter was granted to Huntingdon, conferring the government of the town on a mayor and twelve aldermen appointed for life. To this Cromwell raised no objection, taking no special delight in representative institutions, but he protested against so much of the charter as, by allowing the new corporation to deal at its pleasure with the common property of the borough, left the holders of rights of pasture at their mercy; and, heated by a sense of injustice to his poorer neighbours, he spoke angrily on the matter to Barnard, the new mayor. Cromwell was summoned before the council, with the result that the Earl of Manchester, appointed to arbitrate, sustained his objections, whilst Cromwell, having gained his point, apologised for the roughness of his speech. It is not unlikely that it was in consequence of this difference with the new governors of the town that he shortly afterwards sold his property there, and removed to St. Ives, where he established himself as a grazing farmer. Nor was he less solicitous for the spiritual than for the temporal welfare of his neighbours. Many Puritans were at this time attempting to lessen the influence of the beneficed clergy, who were, in many places, opposed to them, by raising sums for the payment of lecturers, who would preach Puritan sermons without being bound to read prayers before them. The earliest extant letter of Cromwell's was written in 1636 to a City merchant, asking him to continue his subscription to the maintenance of a certain Dr. Wells, "a man

* My argument would obviously not stand if the remainder of the speech printed in Rushworth were held to be genuine. There is, however, good reason to know that it is not (*Hist. of Eng.*, 1603-1642, vii, 56, note).

of goodness and industry and ability to do good every way." "You know, Mr. Story," he adds, "to withdraw the pay is to let fall the lecture, and who goeth to warfare at his own cost?"

In 1636 Cromwell removed to Ely, where he farmed the Cathedral tithes in succession to his maternal uncle, Sir Thomas Steward. Soon after he was settled in his new home, there were disturbances in the fen country which the Earl of Bedford and his associates were endeavouring to drain. On the plea that the work was already accomplished, the new proprietors ordered the expulsion of cattle from the pastures scattered amongst the waters. The owners, egged on by one at least of the neighbouring gentry, tumultuously resisted the attempt to exclude them from their rights of commonage. We are told, too, that "it is commonly reported by the commoners in the said fens and the fens adjoining, that Mr. Cromwell, of Ely, hath undertaken—they paying him a groat for every cow they have upon the common—to hold the drainers in writ of law for five years, and that in the meantime they should enjoy every foot of their commons." That Cromwell should have taken up the cause of the weak, and at the same time should have attempted to serve them by legal proceedings, whilst keeping aloof from their riotous action, is a fair indication of the character of the man. No wonder he grew in popularity, or that in 1640 he was elected by the borough of Cambridge to both the Parliaments which met in that year.

In the Short Parliament Cromwell sat, so far as we know, as a silent member. Of his appearance in the Long Parliament we have the often-quoted description of his personal appearance from a young courtier. "I came into the House," wrote Sir Philip Warwick, "one morning well clad, and perceived a gentleman speaking whom I knew not, very ordinarily apparelled, for it was a plain cloth suit which seemed to be made by an ill country tailor; his linen was plain, and not very clean; and I remember a speck or two of blood upon his little band, which was not larger than his collar. His hat was without a hat-band. His stature was of a good size; his sword stuck close to his side; his countenance swollen and reddish, his voice sharp and untuneable, and his eloquence full of fervour, for the subject matter would not bear much of reason, it being on behalf of a servant of Mr. Prynne's who had dispersed libels against the Queen for her dancing and such like innocent and courtly sports; and he aggravated the imprisonment of this man by the council-table unto that height that one would have believed the very Government itself had been in great danger by it. I sincerely profess it lessened much by reverence unto that great council, for he was very much hearkened unto; and yet I lived to see this very gentleman whom, by multiplied good escapes, and by real but usurped power, having had a better tailor, and more converse among good company, appear of great and majestic deportment and comely presence." Curiously enough the so-called servant of Prynne—he was never actually in Prynne's service at all—was no other than John Lilburne, who was such a thorn in the flesh to Cromwell in later years. In undertaking the defence of the man who had been sentenced to scourge and imprisonment for disseminating books held to be libels by Charles and his ministers, Cromwell announced to his fellow-members his own political position. In life—and above all in political life—it is not possible to satisfy those who expect the actions of any man to be absolutely consistent. Later generations may be convinced not only that Charles was sincere in following a course which he believed to be the right one, but that this course commended itself to certain elements of human nature, and was, therefore, no mere emanation of his own personal character. It nevertheless remains that he was far from being strong enough for the place which he had inherited from his predecessors, and that in wearing the garments of the Elizabethan monarchy, he was all too unconscious of the work which the new generation required of him—all too ready to claim the rights of Elizabeth, without a particle of the skill in the art of government which she derived from her intimate familiarity with the people over which she had been called to rule.

Charles's unskilfulness was the more disastrous, as he

came to the throne during a crisis when few men would have been able to maintain the prestige of the monarchy. On the one hand the special powers entrusted to the Tudor sovereigns were no longer needed after the domestic and foreign dangers which occupied their reigns had been successfully met. On the other hand, a strife between religious parties had arisen which called for action on lines very different from those which had commended themselves to Elizabeth. In throwing off the authority of the Roman See, Elizabeth had the national spirit of England at her back, whilst in resisting the claims of the Presbyterian clergy, she had the support of the great majority of the laity. By the end of her reign she had succeeded in establishing that special form of ecclesiastical government which she favoured. Yet though the clergy had ceased to cry out for the supersession of episcopacy by the Presbyterian discipline, the bulk of the clergy and of the religious laity were Puritan to the core. So much had been effected by the long struggle against Rome and Spain and the resulting detestation of any form of belief which savoured of Rome and Spain. During the twenty-two years of the peace-loving James, religious thought ceased to be influenced by a sense of national danger. First one, and then another—a Bancroft, an Andrewes, or a Laud, men of the college or the cathedral—began to think their own thoughts, to welcome a wider interpretation of religious truths than that of Calvin's Institute, and, above all, to distrust the inward conviction as likely to be warped by passion or self-interest, and to dwell upon the value of the external influences of ritual and organisation. To do justice to both these schools of thought and practice at the time of Charles's accession would have taxed the strength of any man, seeing how unprepared was the England of that day to admit the possibility of toleration. The pity of it was that Charles, with all his fine feelings and conscientious rectitude, was unfitted for the task. Abandoning himself heart and soul to the newly risen tide of religious thought, his imagination was too weak to enable him to realise the strength of Puritanism, so that he bent his energies, not to securing for his friends free scope for the exercise of what persuasion was in them, but for the repression of those whom he looked upon as the enemies of the Church and the Crown. With the assistance of Laud he did everything in his power to crush Puritanism, with the result of making Puritanism stronger than it had been before. Every man of independent mind who revolted against the petty interference exercised by Laud placed himself by sympathy, if not by perfect conviction, in the Puritan ranks.

Neither in Elizabeth's nor in Charles's reign was it possible to dissociate politics from religion. Parliament, dissatisfied with Charles's ineffectual guidance of the State, was still more dissatisfied with his attempt to use his authority over the Church to the profit of an unpopular party. The House of Commons representing mainly that section of the population in which Puritanism was the strongest—the country gentlemen in touch with the middle-class in the towns—was eager to pull down Laud's system in the Church, and to hinder the extension of Royal authority in the State. To do this it was necessary not only to diminish the power of the Crown, but to transfer much of it to Parliament, which, at least in the eyes of its members, was far more capable of governing England wisely.

That Cromwell heartily accepted this view of the situation is evident from his being selected to move the second reading of the Bill for the revival of annual Parliaments, which, by a subsequent compromise, was ultimately converted into a Triennial Act ordaining that there should never again be an intermission of Parliament for more than three years. The fact that he was placed on no less than eighteen committees in the early part of the sittings of the Parliaments shows that he had acquired a position which he could never have reached merely through his cousinship with Hampden and St. John. That he concurred in the destruction of the special courts which had fortified the Crown in the Tudor period, and in the prosecution of Strafford, needs no evidence to prove. These were the acts of the House as a whole. It was the part he took on those ecclesiastical questions which divided the House into two antagonistic parties which is most significant of his position at this time.

However much members of the House of Commons might differ on the future government of the Church, they were still of one mind as to the necessity of changing the system under which it had been of late controlled. There may have been much to be said on behalf of an episcopacy exercising a moderating influence over the clergy, and guarding the rights of minorities against the oppressive instincts of a clerical majority. As a matter of fact this had not been the attitude of Charles's Bishops. Appointed by the Crown, and chosen out of one party only—and that the party of the minority amongst the clergy and the religious laity—they had seized the opportunity of giving free scope to their own practices and of hampering in every possible way the practices of those opposed to them. It was no Puritan, but Jeremy Taylor, the staunch defender of monarchy and episcopacy, who hit the nail on the head. "The interest of the bishops," he wrote, "is conjunct with the prosperity of the King, besides the interest of their own security, by the obligation of secular advantages. For they who have their livelihood from the King, and are in expectance of their fortune from him, are more likely to pay a tribute of exacted duty than others whose fortunes are not in such immediate dependency on His Majesty. It is but the common expectation of gratitude that a patron paramount shall be more assisted by his beneficiaries in cases of necessity than by those who receive nothing from him but the common influences of government."

As usual, it was easier to mark the evil than to provide an adequate remedy. The party which numbered Hyde and Falkland in its ranks, and which afterwards developed into that of the Parliamentary Royalists, was alarmed lest a tyrannical episcopacy should be followed by a still more tyrannical Presbyterian discipline, and therefore strove to substitute for the existing system some scheme of modified episcopacy by which bishops should be in some way responsible to clerical councils. Cromwell was working hand in hand with men who strove to meet the difficulty in another way. The so-called Root-and-Branch Bill, said to have been drawn up by St. John, was brought to the House of Commons by himself and Vane. By them it was passed on to Hazlerigg, who in his turn passed it on to Sir Edward Dering, by whom it was actually moved in the House. As it was finally shaped in Committee, this bill, whilst absolutely abolishing archbishops, bishops, deans and chapters, transferred their ecclesiastical jurisdiction to bodies of Commissioners to be named by Parliament itself. Cromwell evidently had no more desire than Falkland to establish the Church Courts of the Scottish Presbyterian system in England.

This bill never passed beyond the Committee stage. It was soon overshadowed by the question whether Charles could be trusted or not. The discovery of the plots by which he had attempted to save Strafford's life, and the knowledge that he was now visiting Scotland with the intention of bringing up a Scottish army to his support against the Parliament at Westminster strengthened the hands of the party of Parliamentary supremacy, and left its leaders disinclined to pursue their ecclesiastical policy till they had settled the political question in their own favour. Important as Charles's own character—with its love of shifts and evasions—was in deciding the issue, it must not be forgotten that the crisis arose from a circumstance common to all revolutions. When a considerable change is made in the government of a nation, it is absolutely necessary, if orderly progress is to result from it, that the persons in authority shall be changed. The man or men by whom the condemned practices have been maintained cannot be trusted to carry out the new scheme, because they must of necessity regard it as disastrous to the nation. The success of the Revolution of 1688-89 was mainly owing to the fact that James was replaced by William; in 1641 neither was Charles inclined to fly to the Continent, nor were the sentiments of either party in the House such as to suggest his replacement by another prince, even if such a prince were to be found. All that his most pronounced adversaries—amongst whom Cromwell was to be counted—

could suggest was to leave him the show and pomp of royalty, whilst placing him under Parliamentary control and doing in his name everything that he least desired to do himself. It was a hopeless position to be driven into, and yet, the feeling of the time being what it was, it is hard to see that any remedy could be found.

Before Charles returned from Scotland, which he had visited in the vain expectation of bringing back with him an army which might give him the control over the English Parliament, an event occurred which brought to light the disastrous impolicy of his opponents in leaving upon the throne the man who was most hostile to their ideas. The Irish Roman Catholic gentry and nobility, having been driven into Royalism by fear of Puritan domination, had agreed with Charles to seize Dublin and to use it as a basis from which to send him military aid in his struggle against the Parliament of England. In October 1641, before they could make up their minds to act, an agrarian outbreak occurred in Ulster, where the native population rose against the English and Scottish colonists who had usurped their lands. The rising took the form of outrage and massacre, calculated to arouse a spirit of vengeance in England, even if report had not outrun the truth—much more when the horrible tale was grossly exaggerated in its passage across the sea. Before long both classes of Roman Catholic Irishmen, the Celtic peasants of the North and the Anglo-Irish gentry of the South, were united in armed resistance to the English Government.

It was a foregone conclusion that an attempt to reconquer Ireland would be made from England. Incidentally the purpose of doing this brought to a point the struggle for the mastery at Westminster. If an army were despatched to Ireland it would, as soon as its immediate task had been accomplished, be available to strike a decisive blow on one side or the other. It therefore became all-important for each side to secure the appointment of officers who might be relied on—in one case to strike for the Crown, in the other case to strike for the Commons. Pym, who was leading his party in the House with consummate dexterity, seized the opportunity of asking, not merely that military appointments should be subject to Parliamentary control, but that the King should be asked to take only such councillors as Parliament could approve of. Cromwell was even more decided than Pym. The King having named five new bishops, in defiance of the majority of the Commons, it was Cromwell who moved for a conference with the Lords on the subject, and who, a few days later, asked for another conference, in which the Lords should be asked to join in a vote giving to the Earl of Essex power to command the trained bands south of the Trent for the defence of the kingdom, a power which was not to determine at the King's pleasure, but to continue till Parliament should take further order.

Cromwell was evidently for strong measures. Yet there are signs that now, as at other times in his life, he underestimated the forces opposed to him. His allies in the Commons, Pym and Hampden at their head, were now bent on obtaining the assent of the House to the Grand Remonstrance, less as an appeal to the King than as a manifesto to the nation. The long and detailed catalogue of the King's misdeeds in the past raised no opposition. Hyde was as ready to accept it as Pym and Hampden. The main demands made in it were two: first, that the King would employ such councillors and ministers as the Parliament might have cause to confide in; and secondly, that care should be taken "to reduce within bounds that exorbitant power which the prelates have assumed to themselves," whilst maintaining "the golden reins of discipline," and demanding "a general synod of the most grave, pious, learned and judicious divines to consider all things necessary for the peace and good government of the Church." So convinced was Cromwell that the Remonstrance would be generally acceptable to the House, that he expressed surprise when Falkland gave his opinion that it would give rise to some debate. It was perhaps because the Remonstrance had abandoned the position of the Root-and-Branch Bill and talked of limiting episcopacy, instead of abolishing it, that Cromwell fancied that it would gain adherents from both sides. He forgot how far controversy had extended since the summer months in which the Root-and-Branch Bill had been discussed, and how men who believed that, if only Charles could be induced to make more prudent appointments, intellectual liberty was safer under bishops than under any system likely to approve itself to a synod of devout ministers, had now rallied to the King.

It was, by this time, more than ever, a question whether Charles could be trusted, and Cromwell and his allies had far stronger grounds in denying than their opponents had in affirming that he could. After all, the ecclesiastical quarrel could never be finally settled without mutual toleration, and neither party was ready even partially to accept such a solution as that. As for Cromwell himself, he regarded those decent forms which were significant of deeper realities even to many who had rebelled against the pedagogic harshness of Laud, as mere rags of popery and superstition to be swept away without compunction. With this conviction pressing on his mind, it is no wonder that, when the great debate was over late in the night, after the division had been taken which gave a majority of eleven to the supporters of the Remonstrance, he replied to Falkland's question whether there had been a debate with: "I will take your word for it another time. If the Remonstrance had been rejected, I would have sold all I had the next morning, and never have seen England any more; and I know there are many other honest men of the same resolution."

There was in Cromwell's mind a capacity for recognising the strength of adverse facts which had led him—there is some reason to believe*—to think of emigrating to America in 1636 when Charles's triumph appeared most assured, and which now led him to think of the same mode of escape to a purer atmosphere if Charles, supported by Parliament, should be once more in the ascendant. On neither of the two occasions did his half-formed resolution develop into a settled purpose, the first time because, for some unknown reason, he

* See the argument for the probability of the traditional story, though the details usually given cannot be true, in Mr. Firth's *Oliver Cromwell,* 37.

hardened his heart to hold out till better times arrived; the second time because the danger anticipated never actually occurred.

In the constitutional by-play which followed—the question of the Bishops' protest and the resistance to the attempt on the five members—Cromwell took no prominent part, though his motion for an address to the King, asking him to remove the Earl of Bristol from his counsels on the ground that he had formerly recommended Charles to bring up the Northern army to his support, shows in what direction his thoughts were moving. The dispute between Parliament and King had so deepened that each side deprecated the employment of force by the other, whilst each side felt itself justified in arming itself ostensibly for its own defence. It was no longer a question of conformity to the constitution in the shape in which the Tudors had handed it down to the Stuarts. That constitution, resting as it did on an implied harmony between King and people, had hopelessly broken down when Charles had for eleven years ruled without a Parliament. The only question was how it was to be reconstructed. Cromwell was not the man to indulge in constitutional speculations, but he saw distinctly that if religion—such as he conceived it—was to be protected, it must be by armed force. A King to whom religion in that form was detestable, and who was eager to stifle it by calling in troops from any foreign country which could be induced to come to his aid, was no longer to be trusted with power.

So far as we know, Cromwell did not intervene in the debates on the control of the militia. He was mainly concerned with seeing that the militia was in a state of efficiency for the defence of Parliament. As early as January 14, 1642, soon after the attempt on the five members had openly revealed Charles's hostility, it was on Cromwell's motion that a committee was named to put the kingdom in a posture of defence, and this motion he followed up by others, with the practical object of forwarding repression in Ireland or protection to the Houses at Westminster. Though he was far from being a wealthy man, he contributed £600 to the projected campaign in Ireland, and another £500 to the raising of forces in England. Mainly through his efforts, Cambridge was placed in a state to defend itself against attack. Without waiting for a Parliamentary vote, he sent down arms valued at £100. On July 15 he moved for an order "to allow the townsmen of Cambridge to raise two companies of volunteers, and to appoint captains over them." A month later the House was informed that "Mr. Cromwell, in Cambridgeshire, hath seized the magazine in the castle at Cambridge," that is to say, the store of arms—the property of the County—ready to be served out to the militia when called upon for service or training, "and hath hindered the carrying of the plate from that University; which, as was reported, was to the value of £20,000 or thereabouts." Evidently there was one member of Parliament prompt of decision and determined in will, who had what so few—if any—of his colleagues had—the makings of a great soldier in him.

When at last Essex received the command to create a Parliamentary army, Cromwell accepted a commission to raise a troop of arquebusiers—the light horse of the day—in his own county. He can have had no difficulty in finding recruits, especially as his popularity in the fen-land had been, if possible, increased by his conduct in a committee held in the preceding summer, where he bitterly resented an attempt of the Earl of Manchester to enclose lands in defiance of the rights of the commoners. He was, however, resolved to pick the sixty men he needed. We can well understand that in choosing his subordinates he would be inspired by an instinctive desire to prize those qualities in his soldiers which were strongly developed in his own character, in which strenuous activity was upheld by unswerving conviction and perfervid spiritual emotion. He could choose the better because he had neighbours, friends and kinsmen from whom to select. The Quarter-master of his troop was John Desborough, his brother-in-law, whilst another brother-in-law, Valentine Wauton, though not actually serving under Cromwell, rallied to his side, and became the captain of another troop in the Parliamentary army. To the end of his career Cromwell never forwarded the prospects of a kinsman or friend unless he was persuaded of his efficiency, though he never shrank from the promotion of kinsmen whom he believed himself able to trust in order to shake off the charge of nepotism from himself.

The sobriety of Cromwell's judgment was as fully vindicated by his choice of the cavalry arm for himself, as by the selection of his subordinates. If the result of the coming war was to be decided by superiority in cavalry, as would certainly be the case, the chances were all in favour of the Royalist gentry, whose very nickname of "cavaliers" was a presage of victory, and who were not only themselves familiar with horsemanship from their youth up, but had at their disposal the grooms and the huntsmen who were attached to their service. "Your troops," he said some weeks later to his cousin Hampden, after the failure of the Parliamentary horse had become manifest, "are most of them old decayed serving men and tapsters, and such kind of fellows; and their troops are gentlemen's sons and persons of quality. Do you think the spirits of such base and mean fellows will ever be able to encounter gentlemen that have honour and courage and resolution in them? . . . You must get men of spirit, and, take it not ill what I say—I know you will not—of a spirit that is likely to go on as far as gentlemen will go, or else you will be beaten still." The importance of a good cavalry was in those days relatively much greater than it is now. A body of infantry composed in about equal proportions of pikemen and musketeers, the latter armed with a heavy and unwieldy weapon, only to be fired at considerable intervals, and requiring the support of a rest to steady it, needed to be placed behind hedges to resist a cavalry charge. It was a recognised axiom of war that a foot regiment marching across open country required cavalry as a convoy to ward off destructive attacks by the enemy's horse. So unquestioned was the inferiority of infantry, that unless the horsemen who gathered round Charles's standard when it was displayed on the Castle Hill at Nottingham could be overpowered, the resistance of the Parliamentary army could hardly be prolonged for many months. That they were overpowered was the achievement of Cromwell, and of Cromwell alone.

It was something that Cromwell had gathered round him his sixty God-fearing men. It was more, that he did not confide, as a mere fanatic would have done, in their untried zeal. His recruits were subjected to an iron discipline. The hot fire of enthusiasm for the cause in which they had been enlisted burnt strongly within them. They had drawn their swords not for constitutional safeguards, but in the service of God Himself, and God Himself, they devoutly trusted, would shelter His servants in the day of battle against the impious men who were less their enemies that His. It was no reason—so they learnt from their captain—that they should remit any single precaution recommended by the most worldly of military experts. Cromwell almost certainly never told his soldiers—in so many words—to trust in God and keep their powder dry. Yet, apocryphal as is the anecdote, it well represents the spirit in which Cromwell's commands were issued. The very vividness of his apprehension of the supernatural enabled him to pass rapidly without any sense of incongruity from religious exhortations to the practical satisfaction of the demands of the material world.

When on October 23, 1642, the first battle of the war was fought at Edgehill, Cromwell's troop was one of the few not swept away by Rupert's headlong charge, probably because coming late upon the field he did not join the main army till the Royalist horse had ceased to trouble it. At all events, he took his share in the indispensable service rendered by the little force of cavalry remaining at Essex's disposal, when in the opposing ranks there was no cavalry at all. It was the co-operation of this force which, by assailing in flank and rear the King's foot regiments, whilst the infantry broke them up in front, enabled the Parliamentary army to claim at least a doubtful victory in the place of the rout which would have befallen it if Rupert, on his late return, had found his master's foot in a condition to carry on the struggle. Whatever else Cromwell learnt from his first experience of actual warfare, he had learnt from Rupert's failure after early success never to forget that headlong valour alone will accomplish little, and that a good cavalry officer requires to know when to draw rein, as well as when to charge, and to subordinate the conduct of the attack in which he is personally engaged to the needs of the army as a whole.

Many months were to pass away before Cromwell was to measure swords with Rupert. He remained under Essex almost to the end of the year, and was present at Turnham Green, when Essex saw Charles, after taking up a position at Brentford in the hope of forcing a passage to London, march off to Reading and Oxford without attempting to strike a blow. Towards the end of 1642, or in the early part of 1643, Cromwell had work found for him which was eventually to breathe a new spirit into the Parliamentary army. Enormous as was the advantage which the devotion of London conferred upon Parliament, London by no means exercised that supreme influence which was exercised by Paris in the times of the French Revolution. Both parties, therefore, put forth their efforts in organising local forces, but of all the local organisations which were brought into existence, the only one entirely successful was the Eastern Association, comprising Essex, Suffolk, Norfolk, Cambridge and Herts, and that mainly because Cromwell was at hand to keep it up to the mark. There was to be a general fund at the service of the association, whilst the forces raised in the several shires of which it was composed were to be at the disposal of a common committee.

In England generally the first half of 1643 was a time of desultory fighting, alternating with efforts to make peace without the conditions which might have brought peace within sight. It was not to be expected either that Parliament would accept Charles on his own terms, or that Charles would bow down to any terms which Parliament was likely to offer. Cromwell, at least, took no part in these futile negotiations, and did all that in him lay to clear the counties of the Eastern Association from Royalists, and to put them in a state of defence against Royalist incursions. At some time later than January 23, and before the end of February, he was promoted to a colonelcy. In March he was fortifying Cambridge, and urgently pleading for contributions to enable him to complete the work. Again we find him sending to arrest a Royalist sheriff who attempted to collect soldiers at St. Alban's, and then hurrying to Lowestoft to crush a Royalist movement in the town. After this no more is heard of Royalism holding up its head in any corner of the association, and to the end of the war no Royalist in arms again set foot within it. By the end of May it was joined by Huntingdonshire, the county of Cromwell's birth.

Cromwell's superabundant energy was employed in other ways than in contending against armed men. Laud's enforcement of at least external signs of respect to objects consecrated to religious usage had provoked a reaction which influenced Puritanism on its least noble side. A certain Dowsing has left a diary, showing how he visited the Suffolk churches, pulling down crosses, destroying pictures and tearing up brasses inscribed with *Orate pro animâ,* the usual expression of mediæval piety towards the dead. At Cambridge, Cromwell himself, finding opposition amongst those in authority in the University, sent up three of the Heads of Houses in custody to Westminster, and on a cold night in March shut up the Vice-Chancellor and other dignitaries in the public schools till midnight without food or firing, because they refused to pay taxes imposed by Parliament.

Nor was it only with open enemies that Cromwell and those who sympathised with him had to deal. Of all forms of war civil strife is the most hideous, and it is no wonder that the hands of many who had entered upon it with the expectation that a few months or even weeks would suffice to crush the King were now slackened. Was it not better, they asked, to come to terms with Charles than to continue a struggle which promised to drag out for years? Negotiations opened at Oxford in the spring failed, indeed, to lead to peace, because neither party had the spirit of compromise, but they were accompanied or followed by the defection from the Parliamentary ranks of men who, at the outset, had stood up manfully against the King, such as Sir Hugh Cholmley, who hoisted the royal colours over Scarborough Castle, which had been entrusted to him by the Houses; and the Hothams, father and son, who, whilst nominally continuing to serve the Parliament, were watching for an opportunity of profitable desertion. Such tendencies were encouraged by the vigour with which the King's armies were handled, and the successes they gained in the early summer. On May 16 the Parliamentary General, the Earl of Stamford, was defeated at Stratton, with the result that Sir Ralph Hopton was able to overrun the Western counties at the head of the Royalist troops, and though defeated on Lansdown by Sir William Waller, was succoured by a Royalist army which, on July 13, crushed Waller's army on Roundway Down; whilst on July 26 Bristol was taken by Rupert, and the whole of the Southern counties thrown open to the assaults of the King's partisans. Farther east, though Essex succeeded in capturing Reading, his army melted away before disease and mismanagement. On June 18 Hampden was mortally wounded at Chalgrove Field. Lord Fairfax and his son, Sir Thomas Fairfax, were with difficulty holding their own in the West Riding of Yorkshire against a Royalist force under the command of the Earl of Newcastle. By the middle of the year, the Parliamentary armies were threatened with ruin on almost every side.

The one conspicuous exception to these tales of disaster was found in the news from the Eastern Association, where Cromwell's vigour upheld the fight. Yet Cromwell had no slight difficulties against which to contend. When, by the end of April, he had cleared the shires of the association from hostile forces, he made his way into Lincolnshire, and called on the neighbouring military commanders of his own party to join him in an attack on the Royalist garrison at Newark, from which parties issued forth to overawe and despoil the Parliamentarians of the neighbourhood. Those upon whom he called—Sir John Gell at Nottingham, the Lincolnshire gentry, and Stamford's son, Lord Grey of Groby, in Leicestershire, were in command of local forces, and placed the interests of their own localities above the common good. Stamford's mansion at Broadgates, hard by Leicester, was exposed to attack from the Royalist garrison at Ashby-de-la-Zouch, and consequently Lord Grey hung back from joining in an enterprise which would leave Leicester at the mercy of the enemy, and his example was followed in other quarters. "Believe it," wrote Cromwell wrathfully, "it were better, in my poor opinion, Leicester were not, than that there should not be found an immediate taking of the field by our forces to accomplish the common ends." To subordinate local interests to the "common ends" was as much the condition of Cromwell's success as the discipline under which he had brought the fiery troops under his command.

The result of that discipline was soon to appear. On May 13 he fell in near Grantham with a cavalry force from Newark far outnumbering his own. Taking a lesson from Rupert, who had taught him at Edgehill that the horse, and not the pistol, was the true weapon of the mounted horseman, he dashed upon the enemy, who weakly halted to receive the charge, and was thoroughly beaten in consequence. Cromwell, as usual, piously attributed his success to the Divine intervention. "With this handful," he wrote, "it pleased God to cast the scale."

The success of Cromwell's horse was all the more reason why financial support should be accorded to its commander. Voluntary contributions were still the backbone of the resources of Parliament, though a system of forced payments was being gradually established. "Lay not," wrote Cromwell to the Mayor of Colchester, "too much on the back of a poor gentleman who desires, without much noise, to lay down his life and bleed the last drop to serve the cause and God. I ask not money for myself; I desire to deny myself, but others will not be satisfied."

Cromwell once more called on the local commanders to gather their forces, not for an attack on Newark, but for a march into Yorkshire to the relief of the Fairfaxes. Early in June some 6,000 men were gathered at Nottingham. Once more the effort came to nothing. The commanders excused themselves from moving, on the plea that the Fairfaxes did not need their help. One of their number, the younger Hotham, was detected in an intrigue with the enemy. Mainly by Cromwell's energy he was seized, and ultimately, together with his father, was sent to London, where they were both executed as traitors. In Yorkshire the tide was running against the Fairfaxes. On June 30 they were defeated at Adwalton Moor. The whole of the West Riding was lost, and the commanders forced to take refuge in Hull. Newcastle, with his victorious army, would soon be heard of in Lincolnshire, where Lord Willoughby of Parham had lately seized Gainsborough for Parliament. Among the troops ordered to maintain this advanced position was Cromwell's regiment, and on July 28 that regiment defeated a strong body of Royalist horse near Gainsborough. Later in the day news was brought that a force of the enemy was approaching from the North. Cromwell, whose cavalry was supported by a body of foot, went out to meet it, only to find himself face to face with Newcastle's whole army. Though the Parliamentary infantry took flight at once, the horse retired by sections, showing a bold front, and regaining the town with the loss of only two men. This cavalry, which combined the dash of Grantham with the discipline of Gainsborough, spelt victory for the Parliamentary side.

Yet, at the moment, the prospect was gloomy enough. On July 30 Gainsborough surrendered, and unless Cromwell's forces could be augmented, there was little to intervene between Newcastle's army and London. "It's no longer disputing," wrote Cromwell to the Committee at Cambridge, "but out instantly all you can. Almost all our foot have quitted Stamford; there is nothing to interrupt an enemy but our horse that is considerable. You must act lively. Do it without distraction. Neglect no means."

Cromwell knew that more than his own name was required to rally the force needed at this desperate conjuncture. At his instance Parliament appointed the new Earl of Manchester—who, as Lord Kimbolton, had been the one member of the House of Lords marked out by the King for impeachment together with the five members of the House of Commons—as Commander of the Eastern Association, and ordered an army of 10,000 men to be raised within its limits. Whilst in the South, Essex raised the siege of Gloucester, and was successful enough at Newbury to make good his retreat to London, Manchester's new army, in which Cromwell commanded the horse, defeated a party of Royalists at Winceby, compelled Newcastle to raise the siege of Hull, and retook Lincoln, which had fallen into the hands of the enemy. Lincolnshire was now added to the Eastern Association, the one part of England on which the eyes of the Parliamentary chiefs could rest with complete satisfaction.

Sooner or later Cromwell would have to face other questions than those of military afficiency. When Pym and his supporters drew up the Grand Remonstrance, they did not contemplate the introduction of any principle of religious liberty. The Church was to be exclusively Puritan, on some plan to be settled by Parliament upon the advice of an Assembly of Divines. That Assembly met on July 1, 1643, and if it had been left to itself, would probably have recommended the adoption of some non-episcopalian system of Church-government; whilst Parliament, faithful to the traditions of English governments, would have taken care that the clergy should be placed under some form of lay government emanating from Parliament itself. In the summer of 1643 it was impossible to separate questions of ecclesiastical organisation from those arising out of the political necessities of the hour. It was known that Charles was angling for the support of Ireland and Scotland, and if Parliament was not to be overborne, it was necessary to meet him on the same ground. In Ireland Charles was fairly successful. On September 15 his Lord Lieutenant obtained from the Confederate Catholics, who were in arms against his Government, a cessation of hostilities, which would enable him to divert a portion of his own troops to the defence of the King's cause in England; ultimately, as he hoped, to be followed by an army levied amongst the Irish Catholics. Charles's attempt to win Scotland to his side was less successful. The predominant party at Edinburgh was that led by the Marquis of Argyle, who had climbed to power with the help of the Presbyterian organisation of the Church, and who justly calculated that, if Charles gained his ends in England, the weight of his victorious sword would be thrown into the balance of the party led by the Duke of Hamilton. That party however, embracing as it did the bulk of the Scottish nobility, would not only have made short work of Argyle's political dictatorship, bu. would have taken good care that the Presbyterian clergy should, in some way or other, be reduced to dependence on the laity. When, therefore, English Parliamentary Commissioners arrived in Edinburgh to treat for military assistance, they were confronted by a demand that they should accept a document known as the Solemn League and Covenant, binding England to accept the full Scottish Presbyterian system with its Church Courts, claiming as by Divine right to settle all ecclesiastical matters without the interference of the lay government. It is true that this demand was somewhat veiled in the engagement to reform religion in the Church of England, "according to the example of the best reformed Churches," so as to bring the Churches in both nations to the nearest conjunction and uniformity. The leading English Commissioner, however, the younger Sir Henry Vane, was one of the few Englishmen who at this time championed a system of religious liberty, and he now succeeded in keeping a door open by proposing the addition of a few words, declaring that religion was to be reformed in England according to the Word of God, as well as by the example of the best reformed Churches. In this form the Covenant was brought back to Westminster, and in this form it was sworn to by the members of Parliament, and required to be sworn to by all Englishmen above the age of eighteen. Few indeed amongst the members of Parliament willingly placed their necks under the yoke. It was the price paid for Scottish armed assistance, simply because that assistance could be had on no other terms. The alliance with the Scots was the last work of Pym, who died before the Scottish army, the aid of which he had so dearly purchased, crossed the Borders into England.

There were two ways of opposing the Scottish system of Divine-right Presbyterianism, the old one of the Tudor and Stuart Kings, placing the Church under lay control; and the new one, proclaiming the right of individuals to religious liberty, which was advocated by Vane, and was in the course of the next few months advocated by a handful of Independent ministers in the Assembly of divines, and by writers like Roger Williams and Henry Robinson in the press. Like

...octrines, it made its way slowly, and for long ap-... the great majority of Englishmen to be redolent of ...hy. The freedom from restraint which every revolution brings, together with the habit of looking to the Bible as verbally inspired, had led to the growth of sects upholding doctrines, some of which gave rational offence to men of cultivated intelligence and encouraged them to look for a remedy to the repressive action of the State. On the other hand, a small number of men, most of them attached to the Independent or Baptist bodies, fully accepted the principle of religious liberty, at least within the bounds of Puritanism. For the present the question was merely Parliamentary; but it might easily be brought within the sphere of military influence, and it was not without significance that, though Essex and Waller, who had comparatively failed as generals, were on the side of Presbyterian repression, Cromwell, who had shown himself to be the most successful soldier in England, declared himself on the side of liberty. In the sectarian sense indeed, Cromwell never attached himself to the Independent or to any other religious body. In firm adherence to the great doctrine of toleration, which spread abroad from the Independents or from the Baptists, who were but Independents with a special doctrine added to their tenets, Cromwell was the foremost Independent of the day.

Not that Cromwell indeed reached his conclusions as did Roger Williams, by the light of pure reason. The rites prescribed in the Prayer Book were to him a mockery of God. On January 10, 1644, he ordered a clergyman, who persisted in using the old service in Ely Cathedral, to leave off his fooling and come down from his place. But he had no liking for the Covenant, and avoided committing himself to it till the beginning of February, 1644, when he swore to it on his appointment as Lieutenant-General in Manchester's army, doubtless laying special stress in his own mind on the loophole offered by Vane's amendment. The cause of religious liberty appealed to him on practical grounds. How was he to fight the enemy, unless he could choose his officers for their military efficiency, and not for their Presbyterian opinions? The Major-General of Manchester's army—Crawford, a Scot of the narrowest Presbyterian type—had objected to the promotion of an officer named Packer, who was an Anabaptist. "Admit he be," wrote Cromwell in reply, "shall that render him incapable to serve the public? . . . Sir, the State in choosing men to serve it takes no notice of their opinions. If they be willing faithfully to serve it—that satisfies. Take heed of being sharp, or too easily sharpened by others, against those to whom you can object little but that they square not with you in every opinion concerning matters of religion."

It might be that religious liberty would in the long run suffer more than it would gain from military support, just as the principles of Andrewes and Laud suffered more than they gained by the support of Charles. Already the regiments under Cromwell's command swarmed with enthusiasts who spent their leisure in preaching and arguing on the most abstruse points of divinity, agreeing in nothing except that argument was to be met by argument alone. Their iron discipline and their devotion to the cause permitted a freedom which would have been a mere dissolvent of armies enlisted after a more worldly system. As Cromwell stepped more pronouncedly to the front, his advocacy of religious liberty would become well-nigh irresistible.

On January 19, 1644, the Scottish army, under the Earl of Leven, crossed the Tweed. Newcastle was pushed back into York, where he was besieged by the combined forces of Leven and the Fairfaxes. On May 6 Lincoln, which had been regained by the Royalists, was retaken by Manchester, who together with Cromwell pushed on to join in the siege of York. Rupert, however, having been sent northward by Charles, succeeded in raising the siege; and on July 2 a battle was fought on Marston Moor, in which the Royalist army, successful at first, was utterly crushed by Cromwell's skill. Having routed Rupert's horse, he drew bridle and hurried back to the assistance of the Scottish infantry, which was holding its own against overwhelming numbers of the enemy. The King's regiments of foot were routed or destroyed by his impetuous charge. Cromwell had redeemed the day after the three generals, Leven, Manchester and the elder Fairfax, had fled from that which they deemed to be a complete disaster. Before long the whole of the North of England, save a few outlying fortresses, was lost to the King.

In the South, matters were going badly for Parliament. Waller's army, checked at Cropredy Bridge, melted away by desertion; whilst Essex, attempting an inroad into Cornwall, was followed by the King. Essex himself and his cavalry succeeded in making their escape, but on September 2 the whole of his infantry surrendered to Charles at Lostwithiel. Unless Manchester came to the rescue, it would be impossible to avert disaster. Manchester, however, was hard to move. Between him and his Lieutenant-General there was no longer that good understanding which was essential to successful action. Manchester, longing for peace on the basis of a Presbyterian settlement of the Church, could not be brought to understand that, whether such an ending to the war were desirable or not, it could never be obtained from Charles. Cromwell, on the other hand, aimed at religious toleration for the sects, and that security which, as his practical nature taught him, was only attainable by the destruction of the military defences in which Charles trusted. That those defences were the ramparts of the city of destruction, he never doubted for an instant. Writing in his most serious mood immediately after the victory of Marston Moor, to the father of a youth who had there met his death-wound, his own losses rose before his mind. Of his four sons, two had already passed away:—Robert, leaving behind him a memory of unusual piety, had died in his schoolboy days; whilst Oliver, who had charged and fled at Edgehill had lately succumbed to small-pox in the garrison at Newport Pagnell. Yet it was not only to the example of his own sorrow that Cromwell mainly looked as a balm for a father's bereavement. "Sir," he wrote, "you know my own trials this way, but the Lord supported me with this that the Lord took him into the happiness we all pant for and live for. There is your precious child full of glory, never to know sin or sorrow any more. Before his death he was so full of comfort that to Frank Russell and myself he could not express it, 'it was so great above his pain'. This he said to us—indeed it was admirable.

A little after, he said one thing lay upon his spirit. I asked him what that was? He told me it was that 'God had not suffered him to be any more the executioner of his enemies'." Between a Cromwell eager to destroy the enemies of God and a Manchester eager to make peace with those enemies no good understanding was possible, especially as in the eyes of Manchester the prolongation of the war meant the strengthening of that sectarian fanaticism to which Cromwell looked as the evidence of a vigorous spiritual life.

In Manchester the desire for peace showed itself in sheer reluctance to make war. Cromwell fumed in vain against the Scots and their resolution to force their Presbyterianism upon England. "In the way they now carry themselves," he told Manchester, "pressing for their discipline, I could as soon draw my sword against them as against any in the King's army." "He would have," he added at another time, "none in his army who were not of the Independent judgment, in order that if terms were offered for a peace such as might not stand with the ends that honest men should aim at, this army might prevent such a mischief." This attack on the Scots led to an attack on the English nobility, amongst whom the sects found scant favour. He hoped, he said in words long afterwards remembered against him, to "live to see never a nobleman in England." He is even reported to have assured Manchester that it would never be well till he was known as plain Mr. Montague. Manchester persisted in doing nothing till a distinct order was given him to march to the defence of London, now laid open by Essex's mishap.

Manchester's reluctance to engage in military operations was probably strengthened by the knowledge that Vane, who, since Pym's death in the winter of 1643, was the most prominent personage amongst the war party at Westminster, had come down to York, at the time of the siege, to urge the generals, though in vain, to consent to the deposition of the King, and he could not but suspect that the arrival of Charles Louis, Elector Palatine, the eldest surviving son of Charles's sister Elizabeth, on August 30, had something to do with a design for placing him on his uncle's throne. The design, if it really existed, came to nothing, probably because it was hopeless to carry it out in the teeth of the generals. It was only with the utmost difficulty that Manchester's hesitation was overcome, and that he was induced to face Charles's army at Newbury. The battle fought there on October 27 was a drawn one. That it did not end in a Parliamentary victory was mainly owing to Manchester's indecision. When, a few days later, the King reappeared on the scene, he was allowed to relieve Donnington Castle, in the immediate neighbourhood of Newbury, no attempt whatever being made to hinder his operations. In the controversy which followed, Manchester went to the root of the matter when he said: "If we beat the King ninety and nine times, yet he is King still, and so will his posterity be after him; but if the King beat us once we shall all be hanged, and our posterity made slaves." "My Lord," answered Cromwell, "if this be so why did we take up arms at first? This is against fighting ever hereafter. If so, let us make peace, be it never so base." Each of the two men had fixed upon one side of the problem which England was called upon to solve. Manchester was appalled by the political difficulty. There stood the Kingship accepted by generation after generation, fenced about with safeguards of law and custom, and likely to be accepted in one form or another by generations to come. A single decisive victory gained by Charles would not only expose those who had dared to make war on him to the hideous penalties of the law of treason—but would enable him to measure the terms of submission by his own resolves. If Manchester had had the power of looking into futurity, he would have argued that no military success—not even the abolition of monarchy, and the execution of the monarch—would avail to postpone the restoration of Charles's heir for more than a little while.

Cromwell's reply did not even pretend to meet the difficulty. It was not in him to forecast the prospects of kingship in England, or to vex his mind with the consequences of a problematical Royalist victory. It was enough for him to grasp the actual situation. It is true that, at this time, he had not got beyond the position from which the whole of the Parliamentary party had started at the beginning of the war—the position that the war must be ended by a compact between King and Parliament. To Cromwell, therefore, whose heart was set upon the liberation of those who in his eyes were the people of God, and the overthrow of ceremonial observances, the immediate duty of the moment was to secure that, when the time of negotiation arrived, the right side should be in possession of sufficient military force to enable it to dictate the terms of peace. It was his part not to consider what the King might do if he proved victorious, but to take good care that he was signally defeated. Strange to say, the folly of the Presbyterian party—strong in the two Houses, and in the support of the Scottish army—was playing into Cromwell's hands. On November 20, ten days after Cromwell's altercations with Manchester, Parliament sent to Oxford terms of peace so harsh as to place their acceptance outside the bounds of possibility. The royal power was to be reduced to a cipher, whilst such a form of religion as might be agreed upon by the Houses in accordance with the Covenant was to be imposed on all Englishmen, without toleration either for the sects favoured by Cromwell, or for the Church of Andrewes and Laud which found one of its warmest and most conscientious supporters in Charles. Every man in the three kingdoms, including the King himself, was to be bound to swear to the observance of the Covenant. Such a demand naturally met with stern resistance. "There are three things," replied Charles, "I will not part with—the Church, my crown, and my friends; and you will have much ado to get them from me." It needed no action on the part of Cromwell to secure the failure of such a negotiation, and, so far as we are aware, no word passed his lips in public on the subject.

On November 25 Cromwell appeared in Parliament to urge on the one thing immediately necessary, the forging of an instrument by which the King might be ruined in the field. The existing military system by which separate armies, to a great extent composed of local forces, and therefore unable to subordinate local to national objects, had been placed under commanders selected for their political or social eminence, had completely broken down. So well was this recognised that, two days before Cromwell's arrival at Westminster, a committee had been appointed without opposition to "consider of a frame or model of the whole militia." It was perhaps to assist the committee to come to a right conclusion that, upon his arrival at Westminster, Cromwell indignantly assailed Manchester as guitly of all the errors which had led to the deplorable result at Newbury. Manchester was not slow in throwing all the blame on Cromwell, and it seemed as if the gravest political questions were to be thrust aside by a personal altercation. So angry were the Scottish members of the Committee of both kingdoms, a body which had recently been appointed to direct the movements of the armies, that they won over the Presbyterian leaders, Essex and Holles, to look favourably on a scheme for bringing an accusation against Cromwell as an incendiary who was doing his best to divide the King from his people, and one of the kingdoms from the other. At a meeting held at Essex House the Scottish Earl of Loudoun asked the English lawyers present whether an incendiary who was punishable by the law of Scotland was also punishable by the law of England. The English lawyers threw cold water on the scheme, Whitelocke asking to see the evidence on which the charge was founded, whilst Maynard declared that "Lieutenant-General Cromwell is a person of great favour and interest with the House of Commons, and with some of the Peers likewise, and therefore there must be proofs, and the most clear and evident against him, to prevail with the Parliament to adjudge him to be an incendiary". Neither Whitelocke nor Maynard was eager to bell the cat.

Cromwell replied by a renewed attack on Manchester's inefficient generalship. Yet it was not in accordance with the character of the man who had stopped the headlong rush of his squadrons at Marston Moor to allow a great public cause to be wrecked by personal recriminations. On December 9 Zouch Tate, himself a strong Presbyterian, reported from a committee which had been appointed to consider the questions at issue between the two generals, "that the chief causes of our division are pride and covetousness." It is immaterial whether Tate had or had not come to a previous understanding with Cromwell to damp down the fires of controversy which threatened to rend the Parliamentary party into warring factions. What was of real importance is that Cromwell followed with an admission that, unless the war was brought to a speedy conclusion, the kingdom would become weary of Parliament. "For what," he added, "do the enemy say? Nay, what do many say that were friends at the beginning of the Parliament? Even this, that the members of both Houses have got great places and commands and a sword into their hands, and, what by interest of Parliament, and what by power in the army, will perpetually continue themselves in grandeur, and not permit the war speedily to end, lest their own power should determine with it. This I speak here to our faces is but what others do utter behind our backs." Then, after calling for the more vigorous prosecution of the war, and advising that all charges against individual commanders should be dropped, he proceeded to express a hope that no member of either House would scruple to abandon his private interests for the public good. Later in the day, Tate gave point to Cromwell's suggestion by moving that so long as the war lasted, no member of either House should hold any command, military or civil, conferred on him by Parliament. The idea struck root. It satisfied those who misdoubted Essex and Manchester, as well as those who misdoubted Cromwell. That Cromwell was in earnest in proposing to exclude himself is evident. The majority in both Houses was Presbyterian, and if the so-called Self-Denying Ordinance brought in to give effect to Tate's proposal by refusing to members of either House the right of holding commands in the army or offices in the State had been passed in the form in which it was drawn up, nothing short of a repeal of that ordinance could have enabled him to command even a single troop.

That a door was left open was entirely the fault of the House of Lords in rejecting this ordinance on January 13, 1645. By this time both parties in the Commons were of one mind in pushing on an ordinance for a new model of the army, from which it would be easy to exclude peers, whether the Self-Denying Ordinance were passed or no. On January 21 the Commons named Fairfax as General and Skippon as

Major-General of the new army. The post of Lieutenant-General, which carried with it the command of the Horse, was significantly left open. No legislation now barred the way to Cromwell's appointment, but the House thought it desirable to make their action in the matter dependent on the line finally taken by the Lords. On February 15 the Lords passed the New Model Ordinance. A few days later, the negotiation with the King which is known as the Treaty of Uxbridge, came to an end, and Parliament was now committed to the design of meeting Charles in the field with an army commanded by professional soldiers, and withdrawn from local and political influences. In such an army nothing more would be heard of the dangers of success which had loomed so large before the eye of Manchester. Apparently to save the Parliamentary officers from the indignity of tendering the resignation of their commissions, a new Self-Denying Ordinance was passed on April 3, by which members of either House were discharged from their military or civil posts within forty days afterwards. There was nothing to prevent the reappointment of Cromwell on the one hand, or of Essex or Manchester on the other, if the two Houses should combine in doing so.

Chapter 2

The New Model Army and the Presbyterians

THE NEW MODEL Army had been accepted by both Houses and by both parties in either House, because in no other way could the difficulties of the situation be met. The failure of the negotiations at Uxbridge had convinced the Presbyterians—at least for the moment—that Charles would give no help towards the settlement of the nation on any basis that their narrow minds could recognise as acceptable, and if the war was to be continued, what prospect was there of success under the old conditions? Nevertheless, the creation of the New Model was, in the main, Cromwell's work. Men are led by their passions more than by their reason, and if Cromwell had continued his invectives against Manchester, he would have roused an opposition which would have left little chance of the realisation of the hopes which he cherished most deeply in his heart. All through the discussion he had shown not only a readiness to sacrifice his own personal interests, but a determination to avoid even criticism of the actions of his opponents in all matters of less importance, provided that he had his way in the one thing most important of all. Without a word of censure he had left the Presbyterians not only to negotiate with Charles, but to pass votes for the establishment of intolerant Presbyterianism in England. The skill with which he avoided friction by keeping himself in the background, whilst he allowed others to work for him, doubtless contributed much to his success. It revealed the highest qualities of statesmanship on the hypothesis that he was acting with a single eye to the public good. It revealed the lowest arts of the trickster, on the hypothesis that he was scheming for his own ultimate advantage. As human nature is constituted, there would be many who would convince themselves that the lower interpretation of his conduct was the true one.

At all events, the New Model Army was being brought into shape in the spring of 1645. It was composed partly of men pressed into the service, partly of soldiers who had served in former armies. That the Puritan, and even the Independent element, was well represented amongst the cavalry of which Cromwell's troops formed the nucleus, there can be little doubt; and even amongst the infantry, the fact that it could only be recruited from those parts of England which at that time acknowledged the authority of the Houses, and that in those counties Puritanism was especially rife, would naturally introduce into the ranks a considerable number of Puritans, whether Independent or not. The army, however, was certainly not formed on the principles which had guided Cromwell, in the selection of his first troopers, and indeed it was impossible to select 30,000 men on the exclusive plan which had been found possible in the enlistment of a single troop or a single regiment. What chiefly—so far as the rank and file were concerned—distinguished the New Model from preceding armies was that it was regularly paid. Hitherto the soldiers had been dependent on intermittent Parliamentary grants, or still more intermittent efforts of local committees. All this was now to be changed. A regular taxation was assessed on the counties for the support of the new army, and the constant pay thus secured was likely to put an end to the desertions on a large scale which had afflicted former commanders, thus rendering it possible to bring the new force under rigorous discipline, a discipline which punished even more severely offences against morality than those directed against military efficiency.

The higher the state of discipline the more important is the selection of officers; and here at least Cromwell's views had full scope. On the mere ground that it was desirable to place command in the hands of those who were most strenuous in the prosecution of the war, the preference was certain to be given to men who were least hampered by a desire to make terms with an unbeaten King—in other words, to Independents rather than to Presbyterians. In another way Cromwell's ideas were carried out. "I had rather," he had once said, "have a plain russet-coated captain that knows what he fights for, and loves what he knows, than that which you call a gentleman and nothing else. I honour a gentleman that is so indeed." There was no distinction of social rank amongst the officers of the New Model. Amongst them were men of old families such as Fairfax and Montague, side by side with Hewson, the cobbler, and Pride, the drayman. If ever the army should be drawn within the circle of politics, much would follow from the adoption of a system of promotion which grounded itself on military efficiency alone.

For the present the services of the new army were required solely in the field. On April 20 Cromwell, who was permitted to retain his commission forty days after the ordinance had passed, and whose alloted term had not yet expired, was sent with his cavalry to sweep round the King's head-quarters at Oxford in order to break up his arrangements for sending out the artillery needed by Rupert if he was again to take the field. Cromwell's movement was completely successful. He not only scattered a Royalist force at Islip, and captured Blechington House by sheer bluff, but he swept up all the draught horses on which Charles had counted for the removal of the guns, and thus incapacitated the enemy from immediate action. Rupert had to wait patiently for some time before he could leave his quarters.

It is seldom that men realise at first the necessary consequences of an important change, and, on this occasion, the Committee of Both Kingdoms and the Parliament itself were slow to discover that, if the new army was to achieve victory, its movements must be guided, not by politicians at Westminster, but by the general in the field. The first act of the Committee was to send Fairfax with eleven thousand men to the relief of Taunton, where Blake, who not long before had defended Lyme against all the efforts of the Royalists to take it, was now holding out to the last with scanty protection from the fortifications he had improvised. The Committee's orders, necessary perhaps at first, were persisted in even after it was known that Charles had been joined at Oxford by the field army which had hitherto protected the besiegers of Taunton in the West, and that, whilst a much smaller force than eleven thousand men would be now sufficient to raise the siege, every soldier that could be spared was needed farther east. The next blunder of the Committee was even worse. Charles had marched to the North with all the force he could gather, in the hope of undoing the consequences of Marston Moor. If there was one lesson which the Committee ought to have learnt from the campaign of the preceding year it was that it is useless to besiege towns whilst the enemy's army remains unbeaten in the field. Yet when every military consideration spoke with no uncertain voice for the policy of following up Charles's army without remission till it had been defeated, the sage Committee-men at Westminster ordered Fairfax to besiege Oxford. Charles, at liberty to direct his movements where he would, had been deflected from his course, and on May 31 had stormed Leicester. The news shook the Committee's resolution to keep the direction of the army in its own feeble hands. On June 2 it directed Fairfax to break up the siege of Oxford. On thet 4th a petition from the London Common Council asked that, though the forty days during which Cromwell kept his appointment under the Self-Denying Ordinance had now elapsed, he might be placed at the head of a new army to be raised in the Eastern Association. Another petition from Fairfax's officers asked that he might be placed in the vacant lieutenant-generalship. The Commons agreed, but, for the present at least, the Lords withheld their consent. At a later time, when events had rendered refusal impossible, the Lords gave their consent to an appointment for which Cromwell was certainly not disqualified by anything in the Self-Denying Ordinance in the form in which they had allowed it to pass; considering that that Ordinance merely demanded the surrender of his commission, without imposing any bar to his reappointment.

When on June 14 the army under Fairfax found itself in presence of the King at Naseby, Cromwell was once more in command of the horse. As usual in those days the infantry was in the centre. On the two wings were the cavalry, that on the right under Cromwell in person, that on the left under Ireton. Ireton was driven back by Rupert, who, having learned nothing since his headlong charge at Edgehill, dashed in pursuit without a moment's thought for the fortunes of the remainder of the King's army. Cromwell, after driving off the horse opposed to him, drew rein, as he had done at Marston Moor, to watch the sway of the battle he had left behind him. Seeing his duty clear, he left three regiments to continue the pursuit, and with the remainder fell upon the Royalist infantry, and with the help of Fairfax's own foot destroyed or captured the whole body. Rupert returned too late to do anything but join Charles in his flight. Five thousand prisoners had been taken, of whom no less than five hundred were officers, while Charles's whole train of artillery remained in the hands of the victors. That Cromwell had contributed more than any other man to this crushing victory was beyond dispute.

Cromwell, as was his usual habit, ascribed this success to Divine aid. "I can say this of Naseby," he wrote, "that when I saw the enemy draw up and march in gallant order towards us, and we a company of poor ignorant men to seek to order our battle, the General having commanded me to order all the horse, I could not—riding alone about my business—but smile out to God praises in assurance of victory, because God would, by things that are not, bring to naught things that are, of which I had great assurance—and God did it." No doubt, as has been said, Cromwell omitted to mention that the Parliamentary army had numbers on its side—not much less than 14,000, opposed to 7,500. But it was not the numerical superiority of the Parliamentarians which won the day. It did not enable Ireton to withstand Rupert, and the infantry in the centre was already giving way when Cromwell returned to assist it. It was the discipline rather than the numbers of Cromwell's horse aided by the superb generalship of their commander that gained the day. Cromwell, when he wrote of his soldiers as "poor ignorant men," was doubtless glancing back in thought at his own early criticism of the fugitives at Edgehill. The yeomen and peasants whom he had gathered round him owed much to discipline and leadership; but they owed much also to the belief embedded in their hearts that they were fighting in the cause of God.

After the victory at Naseby the issue of the struggle was practically decided. There was another fight at Langport, where Fairfax defeated a force with which Goring attempted to guard the western counties; but after this the war resolved itself into a succession of sieges which could end but in one way, as Charles had no longer a field army to bring to the relief of Royalist garrisons. For some months Cromwell, sometimes in combination with Fairfax, sometimes in temporary command of a separate force, was untiring in the energy which he threw into his work. Charles was full of combinations which never resulted in practical advantage to his cause. At one time his hopes were set upon Montrose, who, after his brilliant victories, expected to bring an army of Highlanders to aid of the royal cause. At another time he looked with equal hopefulness to Glamorgan, who was to conduct an Irish army to England. Montrose's scheme was wrecked at Philiphaugh, and Glamorgan's concessions to the Irish Catholics were divulged and had to be disavowed. On March 31, 1646, Sir Jacob Astley, bringing 3,000 men, the last Royalist force in existence, to the relief of Charles at Oxford, was forced to surrender at Stow-on-the-Wold. "You have done your work," said the veteran to his captors, "and may go play, unless you will fall out among yourselves." Though Oxford and Newark were still untaken, the end of the war was now a mere question of days.

"Honest men," wrote Cromwell to Speaker Lenthall soon after the victory of Naseby, "served you faithfully in this action. Sir, they are trusty—I beseech you in the name of God, not to discourage them—I wish this action may beget thankfulness and humility in all that are concerned in it. He that ventures his life for the liberty of his country, I wish he trust God for the liberty of his conscience, and you for the liberty he fights for." "All this," he continued three months later, in the same strain, after the storm of Bristol, "is none other than the work of God; he must be a very atheist that doth not acknowledge it. It may be thought that some praises are due to those gallant men of whose valour so much mention is made:—Their humble suit to you and all that have an interest in this blessing is that, in the remembrance of God's praises, they may be forgotten. It's their joy that they are instruments of God's glory and their country's good. It's their honour that God vouchsafes to use them. . . . Sir, they that have been employed in this service know that faith and prayer obtained this city for you: I do not say ours only, but of the people of God with you and all England over, who have wrestled with God for a blessing in this very thing. Our desires are that God may be glorified by the same spirit of faith by which we ask all our sufficiency and have received it. It is meet that He have all the praise. Presbyterians, Independents, all had here the same spirit of faith and prayer, the same presence and answer; they agree here, know no names of difference; pity it is it should be otherwise anywhere! All that believe have the real unity which is most glorious because inward and spiritual in the Body and to the Head. As for being united in forms, commonly called uniformity, every Christian will, for peace sake, study and do as far as conscience will permit. And from brethren, in things of the mind, we look for no compulsion but that of light and reason. In other things, God hath put the sword in the Parliament's hands for the terror of evil-doers and the praises of them that do well. If any plead exemption from that, he knows not the Gospel; if any would wring that out of your hands, or steal it from you, under what pretence soever, I hope they shall do it without effect."

No words can better depict the state of Cromwell's mind at this time. Of the religion to which the King and his followers clung there is no question in his thoughts. He would be unwilling to listen to the suggestion that it was to be counted as religion in any worthy sense. Parliament, mutilated as it was, is the authority ordained by God to keep order in the land. For that very reason Parliament was bound to allow full liberty to God's children, whatever might be their differences on matters of discipline or practice. Within the limits of Puritanism, no intolerance might be admitted. A common spiritual emotion—not external discipline or intellectual agreement—was the test of brotherhood. So resolved was the House of Commons to discountenance this view of the case, that in ordering the publication of Cromwell's two despatches, it mutilated both of them by the omission of the passages advocating liberty of conscience.

At the present day we are inclined to blame Cromwell, not for going too far in the direction of toleration, but for not going far enough. In the middle of the seventeenth century the very idea of toleration in any shape was peculiar to a chosen few. That the majority of the Puritan clergy were bitterly opposed to it affords no matter for surprise. As men of some education and learning, and with a professional confidence in the certainty of their own opinions, they looked with contempt not merely on views different from their own, but also on the persons who, ofter without the slightest mental culture, ventured to produce out of the Bible schemes of doctrine sometimes immoral, and very often—at least in the opinions of the Presbyterian divines—blasphemous and profane. Even where this was not the case, there remained the danger of seeing the Church of England—which was held to have been purified by the abolition of episcopacy and the banishment of the ceremonies favoured by the bishops—degenerate into a chaos in which a thousand sects battled for their respective creeds, instead of meekly accepting the gospel dealt out to them by their well-instructed pastors. Richard Baxter was a favourable specimen of the Presbyterian clergy. Conciliatory in temper, he was yet an ardent controversialist, and, for a few months after the battle of Naseby, he accepted the position of chaplain to Whalley's regiment, with the avowed intention of persuading the sectaries to abandon their evil ways. He soon discovered that the greater part of the infantry of the New Model Army was by no means sectarian or even Puritan in its opinions. "The greatest part of the common soldiers," he wrote, "especially of the foot, were ignorant men of little religion, abundance of them such as had been taken prisoners or turned out of garrisons under the King, and had been soldiers in his army; and these would do anything to please their officers." In other words, the sectarian officers could command the services of the army as a whole, backed as they would be by the most energetic of the private soldiers. Nor was Baxter longer in discovering that the military preachers were ready to question received doctrine in politics as well as in religion. "I perceived," he declared, "they took the King for a tyrant and an enemy, and really intended to master him, and they thought if they might fight against him they might kill or conquer him, and if they might conquer they were never more to trust him further than he was in their power; and that they thought it folly to irritate him either by wars or contradictions in Parliament, if so be they must need take him for their King, and trust him with their lives when they had thus displeased him." These audacious reasoners went further still. "What," they asked, "were the Lords of England but William the Conqueror's colonels, or the Barons but his majors, or the Knights but his captains?" "They plainly showed me," complained Baxter, "that they thought God's providence would cast the trust of religion and the Kingdom upon them as conquerors; they made nothing of all the most wise and godly in the armies and garrisons that were not of their way. *Per fas aut nefas,* by law or without it, they were resolved to take down not only Bishops and liturgy and ceremonies, but all that did withstand their way. They . . . most honoured the Separatists, Anabaptists and Antinomians; but Cromwell and his council took on them to join themselves to no party, but to be for the liberty of all."

"To be for the liberty of all" was recognised as being Cromwell's position. There is every reason to suppose that he had at this time little sympathy with the aspirations of those who would have made the army the lever wherewith to obtain political results otherwise unobtainable. In his Bristol despatch he had pointedly adhered to the doctrine that the sword had been placed by God in the hands of Parliament, and for the present he was inclined to look to Parliament alone for the boon he asked of it. What makes Cromwell's biography so interesting is his perpetual effort to walk in the paths of legality—an effort always frustrated by the necessities of the situation.

It is difficult for us, nursed as we are under a regime of religious liberty, to understand how hateful Cromwell's proposal was in the eyes of the vast majority of his contemporaries. Not only did it shock those who looked down with scorn on the vagaries of the tub-preacher, but it aroused fears lest religious sectarianism should, by splitting up the nation into hostile parties, lead the way to political weakness. To every nation it is needful that there be some bond of common emotion which shall enable it to present an undivided front against its enemies, and such a bond was more than ever needful at a time when loyalty to the throne had been suspended. It was Cromwell's merit to have seen that this bond would be strengthened, not weakened, by the permission of divergencies in teaching and practice, so long as there was agreement on the main grounds of spiritual Puritanism. If on the one hand he was behind Roger Williams in theoretical conception, he was in advance of him in his attempt to fit in his doctrines with the practical needs of his time.

Some assistance Cromwell had from men with whom, on other grounds, he had little sympathy. The Westminster Assembly of divines, which had been sitting since 1643, had done its best to impose the Presbyterian system on England, but in the House of Commons there was a small group of Erastian lawyers, with the learned Selden at their head, which was strong enough to carry Parliament with it in resistance to the imposition upon England of a Scottish Presbyterianism —that is to say, of an ecclesiastical system in which matters of religion were to be disposed of in the Church Courts without any appeal to the lay element in the State; though, on the other hand, it must not be forgotten that in those very Church Courts the lay element found its place. The Erastians, however, preferred to uphold the supreme authority of the laity represented in Parliament—as the lawyers of the preceding century had upheld the authority of the laity represented in the King—probably because they knew that the lay members of the Presbyterian assemblies were pretty sure to fall under the influence of the clergy. Selden indeed was no admirer of the enthusiasms of the sects; but his cool, dispassionate way of treating their claims would, in the end, make for liberty even more certainly than the burning zeal of a Williams or a Cromwell.

With the surrender of Astley at Stow-on-the-Wold a new situation was created. The time had arrived to which Cromwell had looked forward after the second battle of Newbury, the time when Charles—no longer having any hope of dictating terms to his enemies—would probably be ready to accept some compromise which might give to Cromwell and the Independent party that religious freedom which the Presbyterians at Westminster found it so hard to concede. It did not need a tithe of Cromwell's sagacity to convince him that a settlement would have a far greater chance of proving durable if it were honestly accepted by the King than if it were not. Yet it did not augur well for a settlement that Charles, knowing that if he remained at Oxford a few weeks would see him a prisoner in the hands of the army, rode off towards Newark, which was at that time besieged by the Scots, and on May 5, 1646, gave himself up to the Scottish commander at Southwell. The Scots having extracted from him an order to the Governor of Newark to surrender the place, marched off, with him in their train, to Newcastle, where they would be the better able to maintain their position against any attack by the army of the English Parliament. If Charles expected to make the Scots his tools, he was soon undeceived. He was treated virtually as a prisoner under honourable restraint, and given to understand that he was expected to establish Presbyterianism in England.

A few days before Charles left Oxford, Cromwell had come up to Westminster to take part in the discussions on a settlement which were certain to follow on the close of the war. He saw his views better supported in the House of Commons than they had been when he was last within its walls. A series of elections had taken place to fill the seats vacated by the expulsion of Royalists, and the majority of the recruiters—as the new members were called—were determined

Independents, that is to say, favourers of religious liberty within the bounds of Puritanism. Amongst them were Ireton, who had commanded the left wing at Naseby, and who was soon to become Cromwell's son-in-law; Fleetwood, now a colonel in the New Model Army; Blake, the defender of Taunton, hereafter to be the great admiral of the Commonwealth and Protectorate, together with other notables of the army. Yet the Presbyterians still kept a majority in the House. They had already, on March 14, secured the passing of an ordinance establishing Presbyterianism in England, though it was to differ from the Scottish system in that the Church was placed, in the last resort, under the supreme authority of Parliament. An English Presbyterian could not, even when we needed Scottish help, conform himself entirely to the Scottish model. It is true that the ordinance was only very partially carried out, but there can be little doubt that it would have been more generally obeyed if the negotiations, which the Parliamentary majority in accordance with the Scots were conducting with the King at Newcastle, had been attended with success.

That Cromwell watched these negotiations with the keenest interest may be taken for granted; but he does not seem to have had any opportunity, as a simple member of the House, for doing more. We can indeed only conjecture, though with tolerable certitude, that he was well pleased with the widening of the breach between the Presbyterians and the King, caused by the determination of Charles to make no stipulation which would lead to the abolition of episcopacy. Nor can he have been otherwise than well pleased when, on January 30, 1647, the Scottish soldiers, having received part of the sum due to them for their services in England with promise of the remainder, marched for Scotland, having first delivered Charles over to commissioners appointed by the English Parliament, who conducted him to Holmby House in Northamptonshire, which had been assigned to him by Parliament as a residence.

At last the time had arrived when a peaceful settlement of the distracted country appeared to have come in sight and, for the time as least, the Presbyterians seemed to have the strongest cards in their hands. They had a majority in Parliament, and it was for them, therefore, to formulate the principles on which the future institutions of the country were to be built. That the country was with them in wishing, on the one hand, for an arrangement in which the King could reappear as a constitutional factor in the Government, and, on the other hand, for a total or partial disbandment of the army and a consequent relief from taxation, can hardly be denied. The great weakness, and, as it proved, the insuperable weakness of the Presbyterians lay in the incapacity of their leaders to understand the characters of the men with whom they had to deal. Right as they were in their opinion that the nation would readily accept a constitutional monarchy, it was impossible to persuade them, as was really the case, that Charles would never willingly submit to be bound by the limitations of constitutional monarchy, and still less to allow, longer than he could possibly help, the Church to be modelled after any kind of Presbyterian system. That he had the strongest possible conviction on religious grounds that episcopacy was of Divine ordinance is beyond doubt, and on this point his tenacious, though irresolute, mind was strengthened by an assurance that in fighting in the cause of the bishops he was really fighting in the cause of God. Yet the controversy had a political as well as a religious side. In Scotland Presbyterianism meant the predominance of the clergy. In England it would mean the predominance of the country nobility and gentry, who, either in their private capacity or collectively in Parliament, presented to benefices, and in Parliament kept the final control over the Church in their own hands. Episcopacy, on the other hand, meant that the control over the Church was in the hands of men appointed by the King.

The folly of the Presbyterians appeared, not in their maintenance of their own views, but in their fancying that if they could only persuade Charles to agree to give them their way temporarily, they would have done sufficient to gain their cause. Early in 1647 they proposed that Presbyterianism should be established in England for three years, and that the militia should remain in the power of Parliament for ten. They could not see that at the end of the periods fixed Charles would have the immense advantage of finding himself face to face with a system which had ceased to have any legal sanction. Common prudence suggested that whatever settlement was arrived at, it should, at least, have in favour of its continuance the presumption of permanency accorded to every established institution which is expected to remain in possession of the field till definite steps are taken for its abolition.

It is possible indeed that the Presbyterians calculated on the unpopularity of episcopacy and of all that episcopacy was likely to bring with it. It is true that not even an approximate estimate can be given of the numerical strength of ecclesiastical parties. No religious census was taken, and there is every reason to believe that, if it had been taken, it would have failed to convey any accurate information. There is little doubt that very considerable numbers, probably much more than a bare majority of the population, either did not care for ecclesiastical disputes at all, or at least did not care for them sufficiently to offer armed resistance to any form of Church-government or Church-teaching likely to be established either by Parliament or by King. Yet all the evidence we possess shows the entire absence of any popular desire amongst the laity outside the families of the Royalist gentry and their immediate dependants to bring back either episcopacy or the Prayer Book. Riots there occasionally were, but these were riots because amusements had been stopped, and especially because the jollity of Christmas was forbidden; not because the service in church was conducted in one way or another. It is sometimes forgotten that the Puritan or semi-Puritan clergy had a strong hold upon the Church down to the days of Laud, and that the Calvinistic teaching which had been in favour even with the bishops towards the close of the reign of Elizabeth had been widely spread down to the same time, so that the episcopalians could not count on that resistance to organic change which would certainly have sprung up if the Laudian enforcement of discipline had continued for seventy years instead of seven.

Whilst episcopacy found its main support in the King, the sects found their main support in the army, and Parliament at once fell in with the popular demand for weakening the army. Before February was over, it had resolved that 6,600 horse and dragoons should be retained in England, but that, except the men needed for a few garrisons, none of the infantry of the New Model Army should be kept in the service. Their place was to be supplied by a militia which, consisting as it did of civilians pursuing their usual avocations for the greater part of the year, and except in times of invasion or rebellion, only called out for a few days' drill, would be most unlikely to join in any attempt to cross the wishes of Parliament. Cavalry, moreover, being, in the long run, unable to act without the support of infantry, the 6,600 horse kept on foot would be powerless to impose a policy by force on the Parliament. As more than half of the infantry, whose services in England were no longer required, would be needed to carry on the war in Ireland, now almost entirely in the hands of the so-called rebels, it was thought that the number necessary for this purpose would volunteer for service in that country, and the rest be readily induced to return amongst the civilian population out of which they had sprung.

Having thus, in imagination, weakened the army as a whole, the Presbyterian majority proceeded to deal with the officers of the cavalry destined for service in England. Retaining Fairfax as Commander-in-Chief, they voted that no officer should serve under him who refused to take the Covenant, and to conform to the Church-government established by Parliament. They also voted that, with the exception of Fairfax, no officer should hold a higher rank than that of colonel; in other words, they pronounced the dismissal of Lieutenant-General Cromwell from the service. It was characteristic of Cromwell that in a letter written by him to Fairfax his personal grievance finds no place. "Never," he writes, "were the spirits of men more embittered than now. Surely the Devil hath but a short time. Upon the Fast-day," he adds in a post-script, "divers soldiers were raised, as I heard, both horse and foot—near two hundred in Covent Garden—to prevent us soldiers* from cutting the

* This is Carlyle's reading, but the original manuscript is torn, and what indications there are show that the words cannot be "us soldiers." But I have no emendation to suggest.

Presbyterians' throats! These are fine tricks to mock God with." Yet, irritated as he was, he gave no sign of any thought of resistance. "In the presence of Almighty God, before whom I stand," he declared to the House, "I know the army will disband and lay down their arms at your door whenever you will command them." His own dismissal he took calmly. Towards the end of March he was in frequent conference with the Elector Palatine who had offered him a command in Germany, where the miserable Thirty Years' War was still dragging on, and where the cause of toleration, apparently lost in England, might possibly be served.

The Presbyterian leaders, Holles, Stapleton, Maynard, and the rest of them, must have flattered themselves that they were at last in the full career of success. To have Cromwell's word for it that the army would accept disbandment, and to see the back of the man whom they most feared, was a double stroke of fortune on which they could hardly have calculated. In their delight at the good fortune which had fallen into their laps, they forgot, in the first place, that there were many officers, besides Cromwell, who mistrusted their policy; and in the second place that, if these officers were to be deprived of their influence over the private soldiers, care must be taken to leave no material grievance of the latter unrelieved. On March 21 and 22 a deputation from Parliament which met forty-three officers in Saffron Walden Church was told that no one present would volunteer for Ireland unless a satisfactory answer were given to four questions: What regiments were to be kept up in England? Who was to command in Ireland? What was to be the assurance for the pay and maintenance of the troops going to Ireland? Finally, what was to be done to secure the arrears due to the men and indemnity for military actions in the past war which a civil court might construe into robbery and murder? In addition to these demands, a petition was drawn up in the name of the soldiers, asking for various concessions, of which the principal ones concerned the arrears and the indemnity. If the Presbyterian leaders had been possessed of a grain of common sense, they would have seen that they could not retain the submission of an army and be oblivious of its material interests. As it was, they treated the action of the soldiers as mere mutiny, summoned the leading officers to the bar, and declared all who supported the petition to be enemies of the State and disturbers of the peace.

Cromwell's position was one of great difficulty. As a soldier and a man of order, he abhorred any semblance of mutiny, and he had shown by his readiness to accept a command in Germany that he had no wish to redress the balance of political forces by throwing his sword into the scale; but it did not need his distrust of the political capacity of the Presbyterian leaders to help him to the conclusion that they were wholly in the wrong in their method of dealing with the army. It was not a case in which soldiers refused to obey the commands of their superiors in accordance with the terms of their enlistment. They were asked to undertake new duties, and in the case of those who were expected to betake themselves to Ireland, actually to volunteer for a new service, and yet, forsooth, they were to be treated as mutineers, because they asked for satisfaction in their righteous claims.

Cromwell, even if he had wished to oppose the army to the Parliament, would have had nothing to do but to sit still, whilst his opponents accumulated blunder after blunder. The House of Commons being unable to extract any signs of yielding from the officers whom it had summoned to the bar, sent them back to their posts. It then appointed Skippon, a good disciplinarian, of no special repute as a general, to command in Ireland; after which, without offering in any way to meet the soldiers' demands, it sent a new body of commissioners, amongst whom was Sir William Waller, a stout adherent of the Presbyterian cause, to urge on the formation of a new army for Ireland. The commissioners, on their arrival at Saffron Walden, were not slow in discovering that the officers did not take kindly to the idea of Skippon's command. "Fairfax and Cromwell," they shouted, "and we all go." The commissioners gained the promise of a certain number of officers and soldiers to go to Ireland; but, on the whole, their mission was a failure. They had not been empowered to offer payment of arrears, and, as they ought to have foreseen, the indignation of the large number of soldiers who complained that they were being cheated of their pay, threw power into the hands of the minority, known as the "Godly party," which held forth the doctrine that, now that Parliament was shrinking from the fulfilment of its duty, it was time for the army to step forward as a political power, and to secure the settlement of the nation on the basis of civil and religious liberty. The idea was also entertained that it would be easier for the army than it had been for Parliament to come to terms with the King, and that it was for the soldiers to fetch him from Holmby and to replace him, on fair conditions, on the throne.

Of Cromwell's feelings during these weeks we have little evidence. From the house which, since the preceding year, he had occupied with his family in Drury Lane, he watched events, without attempting to modify them. In the latter part of April both he and Vane, who was now his fast friend, with a tie cemented by a common interest in religious liberty, absented themselves, save on a few rare occasions, from the sittings of Parliament. The incalculable stupidity of the Presbyterian leaders must have made Cromwell more than ever doubtful of the possibility of getting from them a remedy for the evils of the nation. By the end of April it was known that only 2,320 soldiers had volunteered for Ireland. Then, and not till then, Parliament came to the conclusion that something ought to be done about the arrears, and ordered that six weeks' pay should be offered to every disbanded soldier. It was a mere fraction of what was due, and a soldier need not be abnormally suspicious to come to the conclusion that, when once he had left the ranks, his prospect of getting satisfaction for the remainder of his claim was exceedingly slight. Thus driven to the wall, eight of the cavalry regiments chose, each of them, two Agitators, or, as in modern speech they would be styled, Agents, to represent them in the impending negotiation for their rights, and the sixteen thus chosen drew up letters to the Generals, Fairfax, Cromwell, Ireton and Skippon. As the cavalry was the most distinctively political portion of the army, the writers of these letters for the first time stepped beyond the bounds of material grievance, complaining of a design to break and ruin the army, and of the intention of "some who had lately tasted of sovereignty to become masters and degenerate into tyrants." The House, beyond measure indignant, summoned to the bar three of the Agitators who brought the letters to Westminster; but on their refusal to answer questions put to them without order from their military constituents, sent Cromwell, Ireton and Skippon to assure the soldiers that they should have the indemnity they craved, together with a considerable part of their arrears and debentures for the rest.

There is no reason to doubt that Cromwell sympathised with the soldiers in their desire for a just settlement of their claims, whilst he was still disinclined to support them in their design of gaining influence over the Government. When he reached Saffron Walden he found that the infantry regiments had followed the example of the cavalry, and that a body of Agitators had been chosen to represent the whole army. The result of their conferences with the officers was the production of *A Declaration of the Army,* drawn up on May 16, with which Cromwell appears to have been entirely satisfied, as, while it insisted on a redress of practical grievances, it contained no claim to political influence. If the Houses had frankly accepted the situation, Cromwell and his colleagues would have succeeded in averting, at least for a time, the danger of investing the army with political power.

On his return Cromwell found signs that the Parliamentary majority was even less inclined to do justice to the soldiers than when he had left Westminster. During his absence, Parliamentary authority to discipline and train the militia of the City had been given to a committee named by the Common Council of London. The Common Council was a Presbyterian body, and its committee proceeded to eject every officer tainted with Independency. The city militia numbered 18,000 men, and it looked as if the majority in Parliament was preparing a force which might be the nucleus of an army to be opposed to the soldiers of Fairfax and Cromwell. In Scotland, too, there was an army of more than 6,000 men, under the command of David Leslie—no inconsiderable general—which might perhaps be brought to the help of the Parliament against its own soldiers, as Leven's army had, three years before, been brought to its assistance against the King. Charles, too, on May 12—Cromwell being still absent from Westminster—had at last replied to the proposals made to him early in the year, and had offered to concede the militia for ten years, and a Presbyterian establishment for three, the clergy being allowed to discuss in the meanwhile the terms of a permanent settlement. In the very probable event of their disagreeing, it would be easy for Charles, at the end of the three years, to contend that episcopacy was again the legal government of the Church—especially as he was at once to return to Westminster, where he would be able to exercise all the influence which would again be at his command. On May 18 this offer was however accepted by the English Presbyterians, as well as by the Scottish Commissioners, as a fair basis of an understanding with the King. No wonder that the soldiers took alarm, or that on the 19th the Agitators issued an appeal to the whole army to hang together in resistance.

Nevertheless, when Cromwell reappeared in the House on May 21, and read out the joint report of the deputation, he was able to declare his belief that the army would disband, though it would refuse to volunteer for Ireland. At first the House seemed ready to take the reasonable course, approving of an ordinance granting the required indemnity, and favourably considering another to provide a real and visible security for so much of the arrears as was left unpaid. At the same time the arrears to be given in hand were raised from the pay of six weeks to that of eight. Yet whatever the Presbyterians might offer, they were unable to trust the army, and on the 23rd they discussed with Lauderdale, who was in England as a Scottish member of the Committee of Both Kingdoms, and Bellièvre, who was the Ambassador of the King of France, a scheme for bringing a Scottish army into England. Talk about securing the King's person, which had prevailed in some regiments a short time before, had come to their ears, and furnished them with the excuse that they were but anticipating their opponents. They accordingly proposed to counteract this design by removing Charles either to some English town, or even to Scotland. Their hopes of being able to carry out this daring project were the higher as Colonel

Graves, who commanded the guard at Holmby, was himself a Presbyterian on whom they could depend to carry out their instructions.

Though nothing was absolutely settled, the conduct of the House of Commons reflected the policy of its leaders. It dropped its consideration of the ordinance assigning security for the soldiers' arrears and resolved to proceed at once to disband the army, beginning on June 1. The announcement of this resolution brought consternation to those who were doing their best to keep the soldiers within the bounds of obedience. "I doubt," wrote the author of a letter which was probably addressed by Ireton to his father-in-law, "the disobliging of so faithful an army will be repented of; provocation and exasperation make men think of what they never intended. They are possessed, as far as I can discern, with this opinion that if they be thus scornfully dealt with for their faithful services whilst the sword is in their hands, what shall their usage be when they are dissolved?" Two days later, another writer, speaking of the commissioners appointed by Parliament to disband the regiments, added the prophetic words: "They may as well send them among so many bears to take away their whelps." It was perfectly true. When on June 1 the commissioners attempted to disband Fairfax's regiment at Chelmsford, it broke into mutiny and marched for Newmarket, where Fairfax had appointed a rendezvous to consider the situation. It was not that the mass of the army had any inclination to interfere in politics. "Many of the soldiers," wrote the commissioners, "being dealt with, profess that money is the only thing they insist upon, and that four months' pay would have given satisfaction."

Such an event could not but drive Cromwell to reconsider his position. Whether he liked it or not, the army had, through the bungling of the Presbyterian leaders, broken loose from the authority of Parliament. It was impossible for him to give his support to Parliament when it was about, with the aid of the Scottish army, to restore the King on terms which, whether the King or the Presbyterians gained the upper hand in the game of intrigue which was sure to follow, could only end in the destruction of that religious liberty for the sects which, though without legal sanction, had been gained as a matter of fact. Yet the alternative seemed to be the abandonment of the country to military anarchy, or if that were averted to the sway of the army over the State. Only one way of escape from the dilemma presented itself, and that way Cromwell seized.

Cromwell, it must once more be said, was no Republican or Parliamentary theorist. Parliament was to him mainly an authority under which he had fought for the great ends he had in view. Now that it had sunk to be no more than a tool in the hands of politicians who, aiming at the establishment of an ecclesiastical despotism, could think of no better means wherewith to compass their evil ends than the rekindling of the conflagration of civil war with the aid of a Scottish army and of French diplomacy, and who had proved themselves bunglers in their own noxious work, it was necessary to look about for some fresh basis of authority, which would save England from the danger of falling under the sway of a Prætorian guard. Nor was that basis far to seek. Cromwell had fought the King unsparingly—not to destroy him, but to reduce him to the acceptance of honourable terms. The terms which the Presbyterians had offered to Charles had not been honourable. They had demanded that he should proscribe his own religion and impose upon his subjects an ecclesiastical system which he believed to be hateful to God and man. Was this to be the result of all the blood and treasure that had been expended? What if the King could be won to bring back peace and good government to the land by fairer treatment and by the restoration of his beneficent authority? The call for a restoration of the King to power did not arise merely from the monarchical theories of a few enthusiasts. It was deeply rooted in the consciousness of generations. A few years before it had been inconceivable to Englishmen that order could be maintained without a king, and with the great mass of Englishmen this view was still prevalent. We can hardly go wrong if we suppose that Cromwell shared the hope that Charles, by more generous treatment than that which Parliament had accorded to him, would allow the chiefs of the army to mediate between him and Parliament, and consent to accept the restitution of so much of his authority as would safeguard the religious and political development of the country on the lines of reform rather than on those of revolution. If this, or anything like this, was to be accomplished, the conjuncture would admit of no delay. In a few days—perhaps in a few hours—the plans of the Presbyterian leaders would be matured, and Charles would be spirited away from Holmby, either to be hurried off to Scotland, or to be placed under the care of the new Presbyterian militia in London. The commander of the guard at Holmby, Colonel Graves, was prepared to carry out any instructions which might reach him from his leaders at Westminster. Not only this, but on May 31, the day before the meeting at Chelmsford, a Parliamentary committee had issued orders to seize the artillery of the army at Oxford, and thus to weaken its powers of action as a military force. The situation was one which, by the necessity of the case, must have occupied the attention of the Agitators, and though no certainty is to be reached, it is probable that it was with them that the plan adopted originated rather than with Cromwell. Again and again in the course of his career he will be found hanging back from decisive action involving a change of front in his political action, and there is every indication that, on this occasion too, he accepted—and that not without considerable hesitation—a design which had been formed by others.

Such hesitation, however, was with him perfectly consistent with the promptest and most determined action when the time for hesitation was at an end. On May 31, the day on which the order for seizing the artillery at Oxford was despatched from London, a meeting was held at Cromwell's house in Drury Lane, at which was present a certain Cornet Joyce, who had apparently been authorised by the Agitators to secure the artillery at Oxford, and then to proceed to Holmby to hinder the removal of the King by the Presbyterians, if not to carry him off to safer quarters. For such an action as this the Agitators, as they well knew, had no military authority to give, and for that authority it was useless to apply to Fairfax, who, much as he sympathised with the soldiers in their grievances, had none of the revolutionary decision required by the situation. Cromwell, whose general approbation had probably been secured beforehand, now gave the required instructions, and Joyce was able to set out with the assurance that he was about to act under the orders of the Lieutenant-General.

There is reason to believe that Cromwell's instructions only gave authority for the removal of the King from Holmby conditionally on its appearing that he could in no other way he preserved from abduction by the Presbyterians. When on June 1 Joyce arrived at Oxford, he found that the garrison had resolved to refuse the delivery of the guns, and on the following day he marched on to Holmby with some 500 horse-men at his back. On his arrival Graves took to flight, and the garrison of the place at once fraternised with the new-comers. In the early morning of the 3rd Joyce, followed by his men, was let in by a back door, asserting that he had come to hinder a plot "to convey the King to London without directions of the Parliament". "His mission," he further stated, was "to prevent a second war discovered by the design of some men privately to take away the King, to the end he might side with that intended army to be raised; which, if effected, would be the utter undoing of the kingdom." To this profession his actions were suitable. During the whole of the day he remained quiet, never hinting for an instant that he had any intention of doing more than preserve the King's person against violence. In the course of the day, however, he took alarm at some rumours of an impending attack, and made up his mind, probably nothing loth, that the danger could only be met by removing the King to safer quarters. About half-past ten at night he roused Charles from his slumbers, invited him to follow him on the following morning, and on giving assurances that no harm would follow received the promise he required. On the morning of the 4th, as Charles stepped from the door of the house, he was confronted by Joyce and his 500 troopers. The King at once asked whether Joyce had any commission for what he was doing. "Here," replied Joyce, turning in the saddle as he spoke, and pointing to the soldiers he headed, "is my commission. It is behind me." "It is a fair commission," replied Charles, "and as well written as I have seen a commission in my life: a company of handsome, proper gentlemen, as I have seen a great while." Having selected Newmarket as his place of residence, Charles not unwillingly, as it seemed, set out in this strange companionship. On that very morning, or on the previous evening, Cromwell, feeling himself no longer safe at Westminster, slipped away and rode off to join the army at Newmarket. Both Fairfax and Cromwell declared for the King's return to Holmby, no doubt considering Joyce's removal of the King to be unnecessary, and, under the circumstances, unauthorised. It was only on Charles's positive refusal to return that he was allowed to continue his journey.

It would not be long before the army would have to experience the difficulties which beset a negotiation with Charles. It had first to come to an understanding with Parliament. Before Cromwell's arrival, the Agitators had presented to Fairfax a representation of their old complaints, accompanied with a reminder to Parliament that some particular persons—the Presbyterian leaders were evidently aimed at—had been to blame. In another declaration, known as *A Solemn Engagement of the Army*, these complaints were more forcibly reiterated, with the addition, first of a demand for the erection of a Council of the army, composed partly of officers and partly of Agitators; and secondly, of a vindication of the army from harbouring wild schemes, "such as to the overthrow of magistracy, the suppression or hindering of Presbytery, the establishment of Independent government, or the upholding of a general licentiousnes in religion under pretence of liberty of conscience." That these two clauses were added under Cromwell's influence—if not by his own pen—can hardly be doubted. On the one hand, if the army was to intervene in politics, it must speak through some organ, having, as far as possible, the character of a political assembly; and, on the other hand, it must be made clear to all that its aims were as little subversive as possible. If the Presbyterians would acknowledge that their designs had met with an insuperable obstacle, and would resign power into hands more likely to use it with prudence, the crisis might be tided over without leaving behind it more evil consequences than were necessarily connected with the intervention of an armed force.

Unhappily the Presbyterians were the most unlikely persons in the world to grasp the realities of the situation. They firmly believed, not only that their cause was just, but that the army—without a shadow of excuse—had deliberately, even before the London militia had been reorganised, plotted the seizure of the King's person, with the object of establishing anarchy in the Church and military despotism in the State. Each party, in short, was convinced that it was acting on the defensive; and, in politics, as in all other spheres of life, results are to be traced less to facts which actually exist than to the assumptions relating to those facts in the minds of the actors. Parliament actively pursued its preparations for resistance, planning the formation of the nucleus of a fresh army at Worcester, and granting permission to the City to raise cavalry as well as infantry. The soldiers were undoubtedly right in holding that nothing less than the outbreak of another civil war was impending.

Before the irrevocable step was taken, Parliament sent commissioners to persuade the army to disband on the payment of an additional £10,000. On the 10th, the commissioners finding the soldiers at a rendezvous on Triploe Heath were received by a general refusal to accept the terms till they had been examined by the new Army Council. The army then significantly marched to Royston, several miles on the road to London. In the evening a letter was sent off to the magistrates of the City, the chief supporters of the new Presbyterian military organisation. It can hardly be questioned that this letter represented the ideas at that time entertained by Cromwell, or that in great part, if not entirely, it was written by him. Striving to blind himself to the fact that he was heading military resistance to the civil power, he announced that those in whose name he spoke were acting, not as soldiers, but as Englishmen. "We desire," he proceeded, "a settlement of the kingdom and of the liberties of the subject according to the votes and declarations of Parliament which, before we took up arms, were by Parliament used as arguments and inducements to invite us and divers of our dear friends out—some of whom have lost their lives in this war, which being by God's blessing finished, we think we have as much right to demand and see a happy settlement, as we have to our money, or the other common interest of soldiers that we have insisted upon." Then followed a renewal of the protest that the army had no wish to introduce licentious liberty, or to subvert the Civil Government. "We profess," continued Cromwell, "as ever in these things, when the state has once made a settlement, we have nothing to say, but submit or suffer. Only we could wish that every good citizen and every man that walks peacefully in a blameless conversation, may have liberties and encouragements, it being according to the just policy of all States, even to justice itself." Then followed the practical conclusion. "These things are our desires—beyond which we shall not go, and for the obtaining these things we are drawing near your city—declaring with all confidence and assurance that, if you appear not against us in these our just desires, to assist that wicked party that would embroil us and the kingdom, neither we nor our soldiers shall give you the least offence." Should things proceed otherwise, it would not be the army that would give way. "If after all this," continued Cromwell, "you, or a considerable number of you, be seduced to take up arms in opposition to, or hindrance of these our just undertakings, we hope, by this brotherly premonition, we have freed ourselves from all that ruin which may befall that great and populous city; having hereby washed our hands thereof."

The army marched, and the City at once made its submission. The bare facts of the case told heavily against Cromwell in the eyes of those whose schemes he had frustrated. In May he had protested that the army would disband at a word from Parliament, and had renounced all thought of bringing military force to control affairs of State. In June he had made himself the leader of the army to disperse a force which was being raised by the orders of Parliament. The very words in wihch he, writing in the army's name, had announced his decision must also have told against him. It would have been far better if he had simply announced that the new circumstances which had arisen had forced upon him the conviction that he had gone too far and had driven him to acknowledge to himself and others that obedience to a Parliament might have its limits, and that those limits had now been reached. The line, it would have been easy to say, must be drawn when Parliament was preparing civil war, not in defence of the rights of Englishmen, but to impose upon the country a system alien to its habits with the assistance of a Scottish army. Unhappily it was in Cromwell's nature to meet the difficulty in another way. When most inconsistent he loved to persuade himself that he had always been consistent, and in taking refuge in the statement that the army put forward its claim to be heard as Englishmen rather than as soldiers, he committed himself to a doctrine so manifestly absurd that it could only be received with a smile of contemptuous disbelief. Cromwell, in fact, stood at the parting of the ways. For him there was but one choice—the choice between entire submission to Parliamentary authority and the establishment of military control. No wonder that he instinctively shrunk from acknowledging, even to himself, the enormous importance of the step he was taking: still less wonder that he did not recognise in advance the unavoidable consequences of the choice—the temporary success which follows in the wake of superior force, and the ultimate downfall of the cause which owes its acceptance to such means.

The immediate results developed themselves without long delay. The army, doing its best to carry on the work of violence under legal forms, proceeded to charge eleven of the leading Presbyterian members with attempting to throw the kingdom into fresh war, as well as with other misdemeanours. The accused persons retaliated by pressing forward their scheme for gaining the assistance of a Scottish army, and for bringing up English forces devoted to their cause against the army under Fairfax and Cromwell. Fairfax and Cromwell were too near the centre of affairs to be so easily baffled by specious words. On June 26 a menacing letter from the army made the eleven members feel that their position was untenable, and voluntarily—so at least they asserted—they withdrew from their seats in Parliament. Who could now doubt that—under the thinnest of veils—the army had taken the supreme control of the government into its hands?

Chapter 3

The New Model Army and the King

IN HIS DESIRE to escape from the undoubted evils of military government, Cromwell had the best part of the army behind him. Nor did it, at the moment, appear very difficult to attain this object by coming to terms with the King, especially as the army leaders were prepared to make concessions to Charles's religious scruples. Claiming freedom for themselves in matters of conscience, they were ready to concede it in return, and, for the first time since he had ridden out of Oxford, Charles was allowed to receive the ministrations of his own chaplains, and to join in offering prayer and praise in the familiar language of the Prayer Book of the Church. It was a long step towards the settlement of that religious question which had created so impassable a gulf between the King and the Presbyterians.

The constitutional question remained to be discussed, and the burden of framing terms to bind the King fell upon Cromwell's son-in-law, Ireton, rather than upon Cromwell himself. Cromwell indeed would never have consented to see Charles replaced in the old position, but he was unskilled in constitutional niceties, and he left such details to others. The main difficulty of the situation was not long in revealing itself. Charles, who had been removed to Windsor, talked as if the dispute between the Houses and the soldiers might be referred to his decision. "Sir," replied Ireton, "you have an intention to be the arbitrator between Parliament and us; and we mean to be it between your Majesty and Parliament." It was not that there was any definite constitutional idea in Charles's mind. With him it was rather a matter of feeling than of reason that he could occupy no other place in the State than that which tradition confirmed by his own experience had assigned to the man who wore the crown. For him as for another as weak for all purposes of government, as richly endowed with the artistic temperament as himself,

> Not all the waters of the salt, salt sea
> Could wash the balm from an anointed King.

Under whatever forms, Parliamentary or constitutional, he and no other was to be the supreme arbiter, empowered to speak in due season the decisive word—always just, always in the right. What was passing before his eyes did but confirm him in his delusion. There had been a quarrel between army and Parliament. Where was it to end unless he sat in judgment to dispense equity to both? Against that will —call it firm or obstinate, as we please—so inaccessible to the teaching of facts, so clinging to the ideas which had inspired his life, the pleadings of Cromwell and Ireton would be vain.

Of this Cromwell had no suspicion. He had never had personal dealings with the King, and had little insight into his peculiar character. On July 4 he saw him at Caversham, where Charles had been established, in order that he might be near Reading, now the headquarters of the army. He fell at once under the charm of Charles's gracious manner, and fancied that a few days would bring about an agreement. In full accord with Fairfax, he hoped to establish the throne on a constitutional and Parliamentary basis. Neither Charles nor any of those who were under his influence could understand the sincerity of this purpose. The French Ambassador, Bellièvre, seems to have sounded Cromwell on the object of his ambition, and to have received the memorable reply: "No one rises so high as he who knows not whither he is going." To Sir John Berkeley, an ardent Royalist, Cromwell explained that the army asked only "to have leave to live as subjects ought to do, and to preserve their consciences," thinking that no man could enjoy his estates unless the King had his rights. Probably Cromwell, in his conversation, had emphasised the points which the army was willing to concede, and had minimised those on which it expected Charles to yield. Charles, at all events, was so convinced that the officers were prepared, almost unconditionally, to restore him to his former power, that he gave it as a reason for distrusting them, that they had not asked him for personal favours in return. There can be no doubt that Cromwell refrained at this time from pressing the King hardly. He was present at the meeting of Charles with his children, now permitted to visit him for the first time since the beginning of the civil war. Himself a devoted father, he was touched by the affecting scene. The King, he told Berkeley, was the "uprightest and most conscientious man of his three kingdoms." Yet he was too keen-sighted to be blind to the other side of his character. He wished, he said, that his Majesty would be more frank and not so strictly tied to narrow maxims.

Already Cromwell's apparent devotion to the King's person was not unnaturally drawing forth harsh criticisms from those who failed to understand the essential unity underlying divergencies in his action. Some at least amongst the Agitators were joining the Presbyterians in sarcasms directed against the man who was everything by turns; who had at one time taken the Covenent—at another time accepted the disbandment of the army; at another time again had made himself the instrument of the army in its resistance of disbandment. Cromwell took no notice of such calumnies. He was more concerned with the eagerness of the Agitators to march upon Westminster with the object of forcing the Houses to condemn the eleven members who were again stirring, and of crushing the discontent which was simmering amongst the City population. Happily the mere threat of force had been sufficient, and Parliament virtually abandoned its hostile attitude by naming Fairfax Commander-in-Chief of all the forces in the country. Would it be so easy to deal with Charles? By July 23, *The Heads of the Proposals,* probably drawn up by Ireton—who, of all the officers, was the most versed in constitutional lore—with the assistance of Colonel Lambert, having been adopted by the Army Council, were submitted to the King. So far as religion was concerned, they anticipated the settlement of the Revolution of 1688, leaving all forms of worship—including that of the condemned Prayer Book—to the voluntary choice of the worshipper. So far as politics were concerned, provision was to be made, not merely for making the King responsible to Parliament, but for making Parliament responsible to the people. There were to be biennial Parliaments, elected by enlarged constituencies, and a Council of State was to be formed, to whose consent in important matters the King was to bow. The first Council was to remain in office for at least seven years. How it was to be nominated after that was left uncertain, probably till the question had been threshed out in discussion with the King. The army leaders had yet to discover how little profit such a discussion would bring. Charles was not prepared to abandon his old position for that of constitutional King, limited, as he had never been limited before, by opposing forces. If he had spoken his objections clearly out it would have been easy to criticise him as one who was blind to the forces which were governing events: it would have been impossible to hold him morally at fault. The course which he took could not but lead to disaster. Listening to the army leaders, he yet conspired against them, still placing his hopes on the assistance of a Scottish army, and speculating on the chances of a breach between the army on the one side and the Parliament and the City on the other, which would enable him to grasp the reins of power under the old conditions. "I shall see them glad ere long," he told Berkeley, "to accept more equal terms." He even went so far as to imagine that Fairfax and Cromwell were to be bribed by offers of personal advantage to re-establish his fallen throne on other terms than those now offered to him. "You cannot," he told them, "do without me. You will fall into ruin if I do not sustain you." He was partly supported by his knowledge that though the City authorities had yielded to the sway of the army, the City apprentices were in a state of disquiet and had broken into the House of Commons, compelling the members to vote a series of Presbyterian resolutions in defiance of the army. In misplaced confidence in this movement in the City, Charles entered into communication with Lauderdale, the ablest member of a body of Scottish Commissioners who had recently arrived nominally to urge the King to accept the Parliamentary terms, but in reality to negotiate a separate agreement between the Scots and the King. Charles eagerly closed with their proposals and allowed Lauderdale to send a message to Edinburgh urging the equipment of a Scottish army for the invasion of England. Unluckily for him, mob-violence was a feeble reed on which to lean. The Speaker of the two Houses, together with the Independent members, took refuge with the army, and the army treating them as the genuine Parliament reconducted them to Westminster. On August 6 Fairfax was named by the reconstituted Parliament Constable of the Tower, which though it had hitherto been guarded by the citizens was from henceforward to be garrisoned by a detachment of the army, whilst another detachment was left at Westminster as a guard to the Houses. The remainder of the soldiers, to show their power, tramped through the City, passing out by London Bridge on the march to Croydon—Cromwell riding at the head of the cavalry.

What could be the possible end of such demonstrations? Every time they were employed, the appeal to force was placed more clearly in evidence, in spite of all efforts to minimise it. Scarcely had the regiments filed out of the City when the Presbyterian majority reasserted itself in Parliament. On the other hand, the Agitators raised their voices for a purge of Parliament which would thrust out those members who had sat and voted under the influence of the mob. Cromwell was growing impatient. "These men," he said of the eleven members, some of whom had returned to their seats when the House was under the dominion of the mob, "will never leave till the army pull them out by the ears." "I know nothing to the contrary," he said on another occasion, speaking of Holles and Stapleton, "but that I am as well able to govern the kingdom as either of them." On this, the eleven members left their seats for good and all, six of them taking refuge on the Continent. Yet the majority in the Commons was Presbyterian still, and refused to vote at the dictation of the army. Cromwell's patience was exhausted. On August 20 he brought a cavalry regiment into Hyde Park in order to obtain a vote that the proceedings of the House, in the absence of the Speaker, had been null and void. Under this threat, the majority gave way, and Cromwell, who had the whole army behind him, gained his immediate end. Once more he was drifting forwards in the direction of that military despotism which neither he nor his comrades desired to establish.

The one way of escape still lay in an understanding with the King. With the King, however, no agreement was possible. Charles, hopelessly at fault in his judgment of passing events, stood aloof in the assurance that the strife amongst the opponents would serve but to weaken both. In the negotiations carried on with the army simultaneously with the latest Parliamentary struggle, he fought every point stubbornly. To extricate themselves from this difficulty, Cromwell and Ireton joined in a vote for resuscitating the Newcastle propositions, and allowed Charles to be formally requested to give his consent to those extravagant Presbyterian demands. Charles, driven to the wall, expressed his preference for *The Heads of the Proposals.* Cromwell and Ireton contrived to persuade themselves that he was in earnest, and gave their support to the King's demand for a personal negotiation with Parliament on that basis.

Under these circumstances the Independent party and the army split in two. The greater number of the superior officers, together with the Parliamentary leaders of the party, Vane, St. John and Fiennes, supported Cromwell and Ireton in an attempt to persuade Parliament to open the negotiations asked for by the King. As was not unnatural, there were others, Rainsborough in the army, and Marten in the House of Commons, who gathered round them a new Republican party, declaring it useless to enter into a fresh discussion with Charles, and even talking of imprisoning him in some fortress. Coalescing with the Presbyterians, who wished merely to summon Charles to accept a selection from the Newcastle Propositions, they beat Cromwell on the vote, in spite of his warning that by disowning the King they were playing into the hands of men who "were endeavouring to have no other power to rule but the sword." Inside and outside the House Cromwell was denounced as a mere time-server, who had no other end in view but his own interests. Cromwell's only answer was to urge Charles more pressingly than before to make the concessions without which his restoration to any kind of authority was out of the question. Conscious of his own integrity, he still hoped for the best, even from Charles. "Though it may be for the present," he wrote to a friend, "a cloud may be over our actions to those who are not acquainted with the grounds of them, yet we doubt not God will clear our integrity and innocence from any other ends we aim to but His glory and the public good." Yet September passed away, and Charles had made no sign.

Charles's silence did but strengthen the party amongst the soldiers which aimed at cutting the political knot with the sword. In the Army Council indeed Cromwell was still predominant, and on October 6 it agreed to meet on the 14th, to formulate terms which the King might be able to accept. In the interval everything was done to come to a private understanding with Charles. Charles, however, was trusting to the probable Scottish invasion, and saw in the events taking place more closely under his eyes no more than a chance of discrediting Cromwell and his associates. When the Army Council met on the 14th, the subject of continuing the negotiations had to be dropped. The position was well explained in a letter from a Royalist. "The secret disposition," he wrote, "is that there is no manner of agreement between the King and the army; all this negotiation having produced no other effect but to incline some of the chief officers not to consent to his destruction, which I believe they will not, unless they be overswayed; but cannot observe that they are so truly the King's as that they will pass the Rubicon for him, which if they could do, considering the inclination of the common soldiers, and generally of the people they might do what they would; but they are cold, and there is another faction of desperate fellows as hot as fire."

Almost, if not altogether, in despair, Cromwell sought a compromise with the Presbyterians on the basis of the temporary establishment of Presbyterianism as the national religion, with as large a toleration as he could persuade them to grant. When the House of Commons refused to extend toleration to the worship authorised by the Prayer Book, it was obvious that the scheme was not one which had a chance of obtaining the assent of Charles. Cromwell's hope of uniting Parliament and army in bringing pressure upon the King was as completely frustrated as his former hope of bringing about an understanding between the King and the army. His impotence could not but give encouragement to the other "faction of desperate fellows as hot as fire" to demand a settlement on quite another basis from that on which Cromwell and the other army leaders had vainly attempted to found a Government.

In all his efforts, Cromwell's aim had been to strengthen the chances in favour of the new toleration by intertwining it with the old constitutional pillars of King and Parliament. His schemes, based as they were on a thoroughly political instinct which warned him against the danger of cutting the State adrift from its moorings, had broken down mainly in consequence of the resistance of the King. It was but natural that earnest men should seek new modes of gaining their ends when the old ones proved ineffective. As the years of revolution passed swiftly on, new and more drastic schemes appeared upon the surface, not, as is often said, because in some unexplained way revolutions tend in themselves to strengthen the hands of extreme men, but because the force of conservative resistance calls forth more violent remedies. The misgovernment of Buckingham and Laud had fostered the Parliamentary idea. The resistance of Parliament to toleration had led to the conception by the army leaders of the idea of Parliamentary reform, and now the failure of those leaders produced the plan of founding a government not on institutions sanctified by old use and wont, but on a totally new democratic system. Outside the army, the main supporter of the new principles was John Lilburne, who had been a lieutenant-colonel in Manchester's army before the formation of the New Model, a man litigious and impracticable, but public-spirited and prepared to accept the consequences of his actions on behalf of his fellow-citizens or of himself. During the troubles he spent a great part of his life in prison, and at the present time he had been more than a year in the Tower. He had a large following in the army, and early in October five regiments deposed their Agitators, and choosing new ones, set them to draw up a political manifesto which, under the name of *The Case of the Army Truly Stated,* was laid before Fairfax on the 18th.

The new thing in this scheme of the recently elected Agitators was not that they proposed to fix the institutions of the State by means of written terms. That had been done again and again by Parliament in various propositions submitted to Charles since the commencement of the Civil War, and more recently by the army leaders in *The Heads of the Proposals.* What was new was that they proposed in the first place to secure religious freedom and other rights by the erection of a paramount law unalterable by Parliament; and in the second place to establish a single House of Parliament—all mention of King or House of Lords was avoided—with full powers to call executive ministers to account—a House which was to be elected by manhood suffrage—an innovation which they justified on the ground that "all power is originally and essentially in the whole body of the people of this nation." It was a complete transition from the principles of the English Revolution to those of the French.

Against the foundation of a government on abstract principles, Cromwell's whole nature—consonant in this with that of the vast majority of the English people—rose in revolt. On the 20th he poured out his soul in the House of Commons in a three-hours' speech in praise of monarchy, urging the House to build up the shattered throne, disclaiming on behalf of the whole body of officers any part in the scheme of the party of the new Agitators, who were now beginning to be known as Levellers. It was to no purpose. Monarchy without a King was itself but an abstract principle, and Charles would accept no conditions which would not leave him free to shake off any constitutional shackles imposed upon him. Only four days before the delivery of Cromwell's speech, Charles had assured the French Ambassador that he trusted in the divisions in the army, which would be sure to drive one or other of the disputants to his side.

The immediate result of Charles's resolution to play with the great questions at issue was an attempt by Cromwell and the officers to come to terms with the Levellers. On October 28 a meeting of the Army Council was held in Putney Church, to which several civilian Levellers were admitted, the most prominent of whom was Wildman, formerly a major in a now-disbanded regiment. Fairfax being out of health, Cromwell took the chair. The Agitators put the question in a common-sense form. "We sought," one of them said, "to satisfy all men, and it was well; but, in going to do it, we have dissatisfied all men. We have laboured to please the King; and, I think, except we go about to cut all our throats, we shall not please him; and we have gone to support a House which will prove rotten studs.* I mean the Parliament, which consists of a company of rotten members." Cromwell and Ireton—they continued—had attempted to settle the kingdom on the foundations of King and Parliament, but it was to be hoped that they would no longer persist in this course. Ireton could but answer that he would never join those who refused to "attempt all ways that are possible to preserve both and to make good use, and the best use that can be of both, for the kingdom." The practical men had become dreamers, whilst the dreamers had become practical men. The Levellers, at least, had a definite proposal to make, whilst Cromwell and Ireton had none. Since the appearance of *The Case of the Army,* the Agitators had reduced its chief requirements into a short constitution of four articles, which they called *The Agreement of the People,* intending, it would seem, to send it round the country for subscription, thus submitting it to what, in modern days, would be called a plebiscite, though apparently it was to be a plebiscite in which only affirmative votes were to be recorded. Nothing

* *I.e.* props.

could be more logical than this attempt to find a basis of authority in the popular will, if the other basis of authority, the tradition of generations, was to be of necessity abandoned.

Cromwell, of all men in the world, was reduced to mere negative criticism. The proposal of the Agitators, he admitted, was plausible enough. "If," he said, "we could leap out of one condition into another that had so precious things in it as this hath, I suppose there would not be much dispute; though perhaps some of these things may be well disputed; and how do we know if, whilst we are disputing these things, another company of men shall gather together, and they shall put out a paper as plausible as this? I do not know why it may not be done by that time you have agreed upon this, or got hands to it, if that be the way; and not only another and another, but many of this kind; and if so, what do you think the consequence would be? Would it not be confusion? . . . But truly I think we are not only to consider what the consequences are . . . but we are to consider the probability of the ways and means to accomplish it, that is to say that, according to reason and judgment, the spirits and temper of this nation are prepared to receive and go along with it, and that those great difficulties which lie in our way are in a likelihood to be either overcome or removed. Truly to anything that's good, there's no doubt on it, objections may be made and framed, but let every honest man consider whether or no these be not very reasonable objections in point of difficulty; and I know a man may answer all difficulties with faith, and faith will answer all difficulties really where it is, as we are very apt all of us to call faith that perhaps may be but carnal imagination and carnal reasoning."

Not a word had Cromwell to say on behalf of any possible understanding with the King. All that he could do was to stave off a declaration in favour of the establishment of a democratic Republic, by proposing that the Army Council should reduce into formal shape the engagements entered upon at Newmarket and Triploe Heath. As those engagements had been put forward as demands to Parliament—not to the King, this suggestion at least thrust aside for the time being the thorny question of the possibility of coming to an understanding with Charles. Cromwell's proposal, however, was not likely to secure unanimity. Wildman, on behalf of the Levellers, refused to be bound by engagements which he personally held to be unjust. On this Cromwell asked for the appointment of a committee to examine this question, as well as any others upon which there was a difference of opinion. He pleaded with his audience not to approach the matters in controversy "as two contrary parties." His bearers were in no temper to profit by the suggestion. Wildman threw out a hint that if Parliament were to patch up an arrangement with the King, it would detract from natural right. The expression at once divided the assembly into two camps. Ireton declared that there was no such thing as natural right. Cromwell asked for the appointment of a committee to discuss the questions that had been raised about the engagements of the army. A Captain Audley sensibly urged the controversialists to remember that it was no time for empty disputation. "If we tarry long," he said, "the King will come and say who will be hanged first." Neither Audley's judicious remark, nor Cromwell's words thrown in from time to time in favour of peace, could stop the wrangle, which at least served to draw from Cromwell the nearest approach he ever made to the enunciation of a constitutional principle. Though the Council of the Army, he declared, was not "wedded and glued to forms of governments," it was prepared to maintain the doctrine that "the foundation and the supremacy is in the people—radically in them—and to be set down by them in their representations," in other words by their representatives in Parliament. To conciliate this doctrine with the upholding of the ancient constitution, reformed indeed, but unaltered in its main features, was the problem which the nation solved for itself in 1689, but which neither the nation nor Cromwell could contrive to solve so long as Charles I refused to face the teaching of events.

On the following day, after a prayer-meeting held in compliance with a suggestion from the pious Colonel Goffe, the Army Council met again, to resolve, after long debate, to lay aside the consideration of the engagements of the army and to proceed at once to the examination of *The Agreement of the People.* This determination was a check to Cromwell, who had proposed the committee. It was not long before his prudence was justified. A debate sprang up on the question of manhood suffrage, claimed by the Levellers as being in accordance with natural right, and rejected by their opponents, to whom natural right was a mere absurdity. After a fierce dispute, Cromwell did his best to persuade the meeting to avoid abstract considerations, and to content itself with the discussion of such questions as whether the existing franchise could be in any way improved. His characteristic tendency to look to the preservation of ancient rights finding no scope in any possible scheme for the retention of the monarchy, fixed itself on the question of the constitution of Parliament. Colonel Rainsborough, who, on questions relating to Parliamentary elections, was the chief speaker on the side of the Levellers, proposed an appeal from the Army Council to the Army at large. His proposal found no support, and the Council broke up without coming to a decision.

After this Cromwell had his way. On the 30th the committee which he suggested, and on which both parties were represented, met to consider the points at issue. The constitutional scheme to which its assent was given followed the lines of *The Heads of the Proposals* more than those of *The Agreement of the People.* It proposed reforms, not an entire shifting of the basis of government. Above all, it adhered to the view that the new constitution should come into existence by an agreement between King and Parliament—not by an appeal to the natural rights of man. In the long run Cromwell was justified by the event. On no other basis would the distressed nation find rest. His wisdom so far as present results were concerned was less conspicuous.

The next meeting of the Army Council was held under discouraging circumstances. Charles, who had for some time been established at Hampton Court, had refused to renew the parole which he had given, and it had been found necessary to strengthen his guards. Though there was no accurate knowledge at Putney of his intrigue with the Scots, enough had leaked out to raise grave suspicion, and when, on November 1, Cromwell again took the chair, he called on those present to "speak their experiences as the issue of what God had given in answer to their prayers." The result was distinctly unfavourable to the King. One said that the negative voice of the King and Lords must be taken away; another that he could no longer pray for the King; a third that their liberties must be recovered by the sword. Cromwell did his best to stem the tide. Pointing out, just as a modern historian might do, that there had been faults on both sides, he called on "him that was without sin amongst them to cast the first stone." He then turned to the more practical question of the difficulty of maintaining discipline in the army, if the authority of Parliament were shut off. "If there be no Parliament," he argued, "they are nothing, and we are nothing likewise." Though Cromwell was not yet prepared to strike at the King, he no longer regarded his comprehension in the new constitution as absolutely essential. He was even ready to accept the new democratic basis of *The Agreement of the People,* if there should be a wide demand for it. He must look, he said, for "a visible presence of the people, either by subscriptions or numbers—for in the government of nations that which is to be looked after is the affections of the people." For the present, however, he seemed most inclined to trust in Parliament as the source of authority. On one thing he was clear, that the discipline of the army must not be ruined by such an appeal to the general body of the soldiers in support of the Agreement as Rainsborough had contemplated. "I must confess," he said, "that I have a commission from the General, and I understand what I am to do by it. I shall conform to him according to the rules and discipline of war . . . and therefore I conceive it is not in the power of any particular men, or any particular man in the army, to call a rendezvous of a troop, or regiment, or in the least to disoblige the army from the commands of the General. . . . Therefore I shall move what we shall centre upon. If it have but the face of authority, if it be but a hare swimming over the Thames I will take hold of it rather than let it go."

It was hard, indeed, in those days, to say where the face of authority was to be found, and Cromwell was far from being able to solve the question. The most innocent suggestion made by his opponents was that the army must purge Parliament and declare the King responsible for the ruin of the country. Goffe declared that it had been revealed to him that the sin of the army lay in its tampering with God's enemies, in other words, with Charles. Cromwell struck in with an expression of distrust in personal revelations. He himself, he explained, was guided by God's dispensations, that is to say, in more modern phrase, by the requirements of the situation. He acknowledged that danger was to be apprehended from the King and House of Lords, and that it was not his intention "to preserve the one or the other with a visible danger and destruction to the people and the public interest." On the other hand, he refused to accept it as certain that God had determined to destroy King and Lords, though he thought it probable that it was so. In the end, the constitutional discussion was transferred to a committee.

For a right judgment of Cromwell's character and habits of procedure no evidence exists of such importance as that which has been thus summarised. Here at least is laid bare before us his reluctance to abandon an untenable position, long after it has become clear to more impatient spirits that it has become untenable. Yet his hesitation is not based on any timorous reluctance to act. It arises from his keen sense of the danger of any alternative policy, a sense which will be overmastered as soon as action in one direction or the other becomes a manifest necessity. On November 8, seeing that the Levellers were bent on pushing forward their proposal of manhood suffrage, he obtained a vote from the Army Council directing that both officers and Agitators should be sent back to their regiments. There can be little doubt that the danger was greater than was thus indicated, and that there was truth in a story which charged the Levellers with intending, at this time, to purge the Parliament and to bring the King to trial. On the 11th, at all events, the brave but fanatical Colonel Harrison was calling for the prosecution of the King, and on the same day Cromwell sent to Whalley, who commanded the guard at Hampton Court, to provide against any attempt on Charles's person. Similar warning had reached Charles himself, and on the evening of the same day he quietly made his escape. On the 14th, after the failure of a scheme for the provision of a vessel from Southampton to carry him to France, he reached Carisbrooke, where the Governor of the Castle was Robert Hammond, Cromwell's cousin. Cromwell's first task was to ensure the discipline of the army. His persistent efforts to keep up negotiation with the King had exposed him to the distrust of the Levellers, and it is said that some of them had resolved to murder him in his bed. There was no time to be lost. On the 15th a rendezvous of a third part of the army was to be held on Corkbush Field, not far from Ware, and there could be no doubt that the Levellers would make desperate attempts to seduce the regiments from their military obedience. To meet the danger, a manifesto was issued in the name of Fairfax and the Army Council, in which Fairfax offered to give his support to the early dissolution of Parliament and to a plan for making the House of Commons "as near as may be, an equal representative of the people that are to elect." For the rest, every soldier would be expected to sign a form of adhesion to the General and the Council. Speaking broadly, the conflict was between the men who knew the importance of maintaining the discipline of the army, and those who would reduce it to an armed mob eager to compel Parliament to adopt the democratic system of *The Agreement of the People.* On the 15th the soldiers gathered to the appointed rendezvous on Corkbush Field, where most of the regiments, with more or less reluctance, submitted to their officers. Two, those of Harrison and Robert Lilburne, both of which had been ordered elsewhere, mutinously made their appearance with copies of *The Agreement of the People* in their hats, as well as the motto "England's Freedom! Soldiers' Rights!" A few words from Fairfax reduced Harrison's regiment to obedience. Cromwell, finding that Lilburne's men defied his order to remove the papers from their hats, rode into the ranks with his sword drawn, on which the regiment, with one accord, did as it was bidden. Three of the ringleaders were condemned to death by a court-martial held on the spot, and then ordered to throw dice for their lives. He who threw lowest was shot in the presence of the whole force, and the mutiny was brought to an end.

By this time the weary round of negotiation was beginning afresh. Charles sent up new proposals to the Parliament, proposals which, if he were in earnest, might possibly serve as a foundation for an agreement. It concerned Parliament and army alike to discover whether Charles, who for many months had shown no sign of eagerness for settlement, was now aiming at anything more than an excuse to enable him to gain time for an arrangement with the Scots. So suspicious had the officers grown that Ireton was heard to say that if peace were to be made between King and Parliament, he hoped it would be such as that the army "might, with a safe conscience, fight against both." If we are to believe a story, told indeed only after the Restoration, but which has inherent probability in it, Cromwell and Ireton, having reason to suppose that a letter from Charles to the Queen would be carried by a man who was to stay the night at the Blue Boar in Holborn, disguised themselves as troopers, and waited in the inn drinking beer till the messenger arrived. Then, ripping up his saddle, they found the expected letter, from which they learnt that "the King had acquainted the Queen that he was now courted by both the factions, the Scotch Presbyterians and the army, and which bid fairest for him should have him, but he thought he should close with the Scots sooner than the other." According to another account, the letter also assured Henrietta Maria that she need not concern herself about any concessions he might make, as "he should not look upon himself as obliged to keep any promises made so much on compulsion whenever he had power enough to break them."

Whatever may be the exact truth about the intercepted letter, it is exceedingly likely that Cromwell, in some way or other, received intelligence which confirmed his growing belief in Charles's untrustworthiness. This view of the case is confirmed by the fact that, not long after, the Parliament prepared four Bills, not as a basis of a settlement, but as a test to show whether Charles was in earnest or not, principally by asking him to abandon his control over the militia. On the other hand Charles so misconceived his position as to send Berkeley to Fairfax with a request that he would support him in asking for a personal treaty unfettered by any conditions whatsoever. When, on November 28, Berkeley arrived at head-quarters, Fairfax briefly referred him to Parliament, whilst neither Cromwell nor Ireton would enter into conversation with him. To the soldiers who had mistrusted him Cromwell professed "that the glories of this world had so dazzled his eyes that he could not discern clearly the great works the Lord was doing; that he was resolved to humble himself, and desired the prayers of the saints, that God would be pleased to forgive his self-seeking." On the following morning he sent a message to Berkeley in a more worldly strain, bidding him "be assured he would serve His Majesty as long as he could do it without his own ruin, but desired that he would not expect that he should perish for his sake." Such at least was the form given to the message by Berkeley when he wrote his Memoirs at a later date, and we may at least take it as established that Cromwell made it clear to Charles that, after what had happened, it was perfectly hopeless to expect the army to bring pressure on Parliament in his favour.

Charles turned to the Scots. There were two parties in Scotland—the party of the ministers of the Kirk, headed by the Marquis of Argyle, and the party of the nobility, headed by the Duke of Hamilton, of which the leading members were the Duke's brother, the Earl of Lanark, and the Earl of Lauderdale, both of whom, like many other Scottish nobles, had thrown themselves into the Presbyterian movement so long as it was directed against bishops, but had rallied to the Crown as soon as the Ministers strove to make themselves independent of the nobility. It was this latter party that was represented by the Scottish Commissioners in England, and on December 26 Charles signed an agreement with them—*The Engagement,* as it was called—which gave him his own way in England, allowing him to put an end to all toleration of the sects, and to grant a dominant position to Presbyterians for three years only. Against the English Parliament and the army the Scots were to claim for the Crown the power over the militia, the control over the Great Seal, the bestowal of honours and offices, the choice of Privy Councillors, and the negative voice in Parliament. In support of this settlement, which included a disbandment of the army and a dissolution of Parliament, a Scottish army was to march into England. Of all the Scotsmen embarked in this scheme, the only man of marked ability was Lauderdale, and though no direct evidence exists on the subject, it seems likely enough that the Engagement was mainly, if not altogether, his work. If the suggestion be accepted that the picture by Janssen in the possession of the present Duke, in which a paper is being handed by Lauderdale to Lanark, represents the transference of the Engagement from the former to the latter, it would lend additional strength to the supposition founded on the relative intellectual powers of the two men. However this may be, it is certain that two days after the signature of *The Engagement,* Charles rejected the Four Bills which had been laid before him by the English Parliament, thus showing his own belief that it was no longer needful for him to keep up even the semblance of an understanding with the Houses at Westminster.

That the result of a successful Scottish invasion would be to restore Charles to the throne on the old conditions, and to sweep away everything for which any English party had struggled, can hardly be doubted. It is true that *The Engagement* was buried in the garden of Carisbrooke Castle, and that not a word of its contents reached any English ears. Yet from the rejection of the Four Bills, following on the visit of the Scottish Commissioners to Carisbrooke, it was evident that some dangerous project was on foot, and even those who had welcomed a Scottish army in 1643, when it invaded England at their bidding, were likely to be scandalised at the intervention of another Scottish army in opposition to themselves. To Cromwell and to the soldiers of every grade, the prospect of seeing those objects for which they had shed their blood wrenched from them by a Scottish invasion, was peculiarly offensive. In the army all quarrels were hushed and all offences pardoned in face of the obvious danger. What was more, the leading officers assured Parliament that the army might be relied upon against the invaders. The extreme Levellers indeed continued to regard Cromwell as a time-server and a hypocrite, and some even of those who were ready to accept his co-operation were somewhat suspicious. "If you prove not an honest man," said Hazlerigg to him, "I will never trust a fellow with a great nose for your sake."

Under the circumstances Charles's Royalist friends were sent away from Carisbrooke, and he himself, after a futile attempt to escape, treated as a prisoner under lock and key. A vote that no further addresses should be made to the King passed the Commons. For some time the Lords refused their concurrence, and it was only on a threat of the intervention of the army that they gave way. After the struggle was at an end, two regiments occupied Whitehall and the Mews. The supremacy of the army in the State was growing more pronounced as each political difficulty arose. There are good reasons for believing that before the end of January, 1648, Cromwell, to whom the interference of the army in politics was almost as objectionable as the establishment of a democracy on abstract principles, proposed to transfer the Crown from Charles to the Prince of Wales; preserving the office whilst changing the persons. No proposal could have been more statesmanlike; but, unhappily, it was not possible to carry it into effect. The whole of the Royal family was too exasperated against the enemies of its head to lend itself to such a transaction. There can be no doubt that Cromwell had, by this time, abandoned all thought of looking to Charles as the basis of the political settlement he desired. About the end of February a letter from Charles to the Queen was intercepted which convinced those into whose hands it fell that the writer was preparing to take the aggressive against his opponents. Early in February Cromwell was found amongst the supporters of a Parliamentary declaration intended to uphold the vote of No Addresses, in which Charles's misdemeanours were set forth at length, somewhat in the fashion of the Grand Remonstrance. His attempt to bring into England Germans, Spaniards, Frenchmen, Lorrainers, and Danes as well as Irishmen was one of the principal counts against him. Cromwell is even said to have "made a severe invective against monarchical government," though it is probable that his argument was directed less against a hereditary chief-magistracy bound by constitutional limitations than against a system under which the King retained the ultimate decision of all questions in his own hands. At all events, he refused to commit himself absolutely to Republicanism, thereby exasperating those who, like Marten, and even his own bosom friend—the younger Vane—had come to the conclusion that, in the England of that day, a Republic was the only alternative to an absolute monarchy.

It was about this time that a meeting took place, the proceedings at which were recorded by Edmund Ludlow, himself a Republican or Commonwealth's-man—to use the term in use amongst contemporaries. Anxious to bring men of different opinions into line against Charles, Cromwell gave a dinner to the leaders of the various parties, after which a conference was held in which, according to Ludlow, Cromwell and his friends "kept themselves in the clouds, and would not declare their judgments either for a monarchical, aristocratical or democratical government, maintaining that any of them might be good in themselves, or for us according as Providence should direct us." The old difference of opinion between the men of practice and the men of theory was, on this occasion, aggravated by the fact that many theoretical upholders of a Commonwealth drew the very practical conclusion that not only were Charles's subjects absolved from their allegiance, but that it was the duty of Parliament to call the King to account for the blood that had been shed in England in consequence of his misdeeds. The conference begun in the interests of peace bade fair to lead to open division, and Cromwell, to silence angry vituperation, flung a cushion at Ludlow's head and ran downstairs. Ludlow in his turn threw the cushion back at Cromwell, and, as he proudly boasted, "made him hasten down faster than he desired." A rough piece of horseplay, it at all events served its purpose in quieting a strife which, every minute that it lasted, was doing injury to the cause which Cromwell desired to serve.

At no time did Cromwell fix beforehand the methods by

which he intended to work, though he never had any doubt of the object against which his energies were to be directed. He had contended first against irresponsible monarchical power, then in turn against military anarchy, Presbyterian tyranny, the political supremacy of the army, and abstract theories of government. He was ready to meet each danger as it arose, with the help of all who, whatever their opinions on other points might be, were ready to join him in attacking the abuse which he wished at the time to abate. If, like Ludlow, they persisted in looking too far ahead, there was nothing for it but to silence them, if it were but by flinging cushions at their heads.

In the Spring of 1648 Cromwell and his political allies had thus to deal with a very complicated situation. They had to face not merely Charles's intrigue with the Scots, but also the widely spread discontent in England. Especially in the towns, men were weary of military dictation, and of the increased taxation by which the army was supported. Parliament too was as unpopular as the army. Englishmen were no less weary of the prolonged uncertainty which neither army nor Parliament seemed capable of bringing to an end. In their longing for a settled government, a considerable part of the population turned their eyes to the throne, as the ancient basis of authority and order. If England had been polled, there would probably have been a large majority in favour of Charles's restoration to power, and yet, it was precisely amongst those whose system was most democratic that the most intense opposition to a restoration was to be found.

To Cromwell, man of order and discipline as he was, a restoration unaccompanied with security against the old mischief was intolerable. Of his own disinterestedness he gave at this time undeniable proof. Parliament having granted him lands valued at £1,680 a year, proceeded to reduce his pay at the same time that it reduced that of other officers, by the large sum of £1,825. Far from taking umbrage at this diminution of his income, he presented not less than £5,000 to the public cause, and also abandoned the arrears due to him, which at that time amounted to £1,500. Certainly dangers were gathering thickly. An intercepted letter from the King's agent at the Hague disclosed Charles's expectation to be succoured not only by an Irish army but by a Dutch one. Common prudence taught Cromwell to do everything in his power to conciliate any party that might stand by his side against so extensive a combination. When his scheme for placing the Prince of Wales on the throne was revived about the middle of March, some of the Episcopal clergy preferred an understanding with the army to an understanding with the Scots. Towards the end of the month, Cromwell was still in negotiation with members of the Royalist party, the purport of which it is impossible to define, but which probably had its rise in his persistent desire to maintain royalty in some shape or form as a basis of order. It is at least certain that he gained much obloquy from his own party. "I know," he wrote to a friend, "God has been above all ill reports, and will in His own time vindicate me. I have no cause to complain." It was never Cromwell's way to answer calumny by a public explanation of his conduct.

At last, however, Cromwell came to the conclusion that nothing was to be hoped from an understanding with the Royalists; and it therefore became more necessary to secure the co-operation of the English Presbyterians. An attempt to win the City Magistrates by concessions was, however, promptly repulsed. On April 6 it became known in London that Charles had all but succeeded in effecting his escape, and on the 9th a City mob was rushing westwards along the Strand with the intention of overpowering the soldiers at Whitehall and the Mews. A charge of cavalry ordered by Cromwell drove them back, but it was not till the following day that the tumult was suppressed. All this while the Hamilton party, which was keen for an invasion of England, was gaining strength in Scotland. So black did the outlook become that one more appeal was made to the King, and there are strong reasons for believing that he was warned that, if he persisted in refusing compliance to the demands made upon him—whatever they may have been—Parliament would proceed, on April 24, to depose him, and to crown the Duke of York, who was still in their hands, as James II. Charles replied by sanctioning a plan for his son's escape, and before the appointed day arrived the boy was well on his way to the Continent.

The first resistance to Parliament came from an unexpected quarter. As early as on February 22, Colonel Poyer, the Governor of Pembroke Castle, had refused to deliver up his charge till his arrears had been paid, and on March 23 he had proceeded to seize the town. At first no more than a local difficulty was apprehended, and Colonel Horton was despatched to suppress the rising. On his arrival he wrote that he was likely to have the whole of South Wales on his hands. Almost at the same time it was known at Westminster that a Scottish army was actually to be raised. Presbyterian as was the majority of the English Parliament, it had no mind to have even its favourite religion established by an invading army of Scots, especially as that army would be the army of the Scottish nobility, who were supposed not to feel any warm attachment to the Presbyterian cause except so far as their own interests were connected with it. It was the hesitation of the English Presbyterians between their political and their ecclesiastical aims which alone could have given a free hand to Fairfax and Cromwell. It was Cromwell who, seconded by Vane, carried a vote in the House for granting concessions which the City, under the pressure of the recent intelligence, was now prepared to accept as satisfactory. A further vote that the House would not alter the fundamental government of the kingdom by King, Lords and Commons, was supported by the leading Independents. The House then proceeded to declare itself ready to concur in a settlement on the ground of the propositions laid before the King at Hampton Court, that is to say, on the ground of the establishment of Presbyterianism without any liberty of conscience whatsoever. Whether Cromwell was in his place when the last two votes were taken is uncertain. At all events we can hardly be wrong in supposing that he had no objection to the Presbyterians amusing themselves with another hopeless negotiation whilst the army took the field. He had had too much experience of Charles's character as a diplomatist to imagine that he was likely to aim at anything more than hoodwinking his opponents till the time came when he might deem it advisable to hoodwink his allies.

Cromwell's presence was imperatively needed at head-quarters, which were now established at Windsor. He found the army in an agitated condition, and we may well believe that his own feelings were no less agitated. The peaceful settlement which he had so long pursued seemed farther off than ever, and he can have brought with him no friendly thoughts of a King who would neither accept reasonable terms for himself, nor abdicate in favour of those who would. On April 29 the chief men of the army held a prayer-meeting to inquire "into the causes of that sad dispensation," and in a discussion which followed on the 30th Cromwell urged those present thoroughly to consider their actions as an army and their conduct as private Christians, that they might discover the cause of "such sad rebukes" as were upon them by reason of their iniquities. That day no definite result was arrived at, but on the next, news having arrived that the forces in Wales had suffered a check, Fairfax ordered Cromwell to take the command in those parts. Before Cromwell set out for his new command one more meeting was held. "Presently," we are told by one who was present, "we were led and helped to a clear agreement amongst ourselves, not any dissenting, that it was the duty of our day, with the forces we had, to go out and fight against those potent enemies which that year in all places appeared against us, with humble confidence, in the name of the Lord only, that we should destroy them; also enabling us then, after serious seeking His face, to come to a very clear and joint resolution on many grounds at large then debated amongst us, that it was our duty, if ever the Lord brought us back again in peace, to call Charles Stuart, that man of blood, to an account for the blood he had shed and mischief he had done to his utmost against the Lord's cause and people in these poor nations."

To what other conclusion could these men possibly come? How were they likely to recognise the deeply seated belief in the justice of his Church and cause which lay behind the slippery trickiness of Charles? and how, even if they had recognised it, could they have counted it to him for righteousness? For many a month Cromwell had staved off this decision. Now, he could not reconcile it to his conscience to stave it off any longer; his conscience in this, no doubt concurring with his interests. He left the Presbyterians at Westminster to their own devices—to pass an ordinance which imposed the bitterest penalties on heresy, and to toy with the idea of a fresh negotiation with Charles, content that they had been brought into line with the army in opposition to a Cavalier insurrection at home and a Scottish invasion from abroad. Every indication served to convince the Houses of the Royalist character of the insurrection. There were tumults either actually breaking out or threatened in Suffolk, in Essex and in Surrey, and in every case a resolution to support the King was either declared or implied. Such a development was no more to the taste of the Presbyterians than to that of the soldiers, and the army was therefore able to calculate on the support of a Parliament which, though it might detest the principles of the soldiers, was unable to dispense with their services.

That army was not one to be easily defeated. Before Cromwell reached his appointed station, he heard that Horton had overcome the Welshmen at St. Fagans. The political effect of the victory was immense. "To observe the strange alteration," wrote a London Independent to a friend in the army, "the defeating of the Welsh hath made in all sorts is admirable. The disaffected to the army of the religious Presbyterians now fawn upon them—partly for fear of you, and partly in that they think you will keep down the Royal party which threatened them, in their doors, in the streets, to their faces with destruction, and put no difference between Presbyterian and Independent." On May 19 the Common Council of the City declared its readiness to live and die with the Parliament, at the same time requesting that a fresh negotiation should be opened with the King—a proposal which was at once accepted. The Royalists were bitterly disappointed. "How long," jibed one of them, "halt ye between two opinions? If Mammon be God, serve him; if the Lord be God, serve Him. If Fairfax be King, serve him; if Charles be King, restore him." To Fairfax and Cromwell the decision of the City must have come as a great relief. The work before them was hard enough, but there was no longer reason to despair.

So far as Fairfax was concerned, it had been intended that

he should march against the Scots whilst Cromwell marched into Wales. A rising in Kent, followed by the defection of part of the navy, frustrated this design. On June 1 Fairfax defeated the Kentish Royalists at Maidstone, but a part of their forces crossing the Thames threw themselves into Essex in the hope of rallying the Royalists of the eastern counties to their side. Fairfax after a magnificently rapid march penned them into Colchester, where they could only be reduced by a long and tedious blockade. At the same time Cromwell, having pushed on through South Wales, was occupied with the siege of Pembroke Castle, which did not surrender till July 11, thus leaving full time for the completion of the Scottish preparations. "I pray God," he had written to Fairfax whilst as yet the issue was undecided, "teach this nation and those that are over us, and your Excellency and all us that are under you, what the mind of God may be in all this, and what our duty is. Surely it is not that the poor godly people of this kingdom should still be made the object of wrath and anger, nor that our God would have our necks under a yoke of bondage; for these things that have lately come to pass have been the wonderful works of God breaking the rod of the oppressor as in the day of Midian, not with garments much rolled in blood, but by the terror of the Lord, who will yet save His people and confound His enemies."

What a light is thrown upon Cromwell's thoughts by these words! No Parliamentary supremacy or rule of the majority—not even a general toleration after the fashion of Roger Williams or Milton was uppermost in his mind. Security for those whom he styled "the poor godly people" was the main object of his striving, though he was too large-minded not to assign an important, if but a secondary place, to questions relating to the fall or preservation of Kings and Parliaments, as the institutional framework of political order without which even "the poor godly people" could not enter the haven of safety.

Three days before Cromwell was released from Pembroke the Scottish army under the Duke of Hamilton had crossed the Border, sending before it a declaration against toleration either for the Common Prayer Book or for the worship of the sects. It was unlikely that if Charles were restored by Hamilton's means he would be required to fulfil more than that portion of the declaration which related to the repression of the sects. The Hamilton party, as the secular party in Scotland, was devoid of enthusiasm, and anxious to throw off the yoke of the clergy. Hamilton, however, was a most incompetent general. He and his army, in short, had no advantage but that of numbers over the well-disciplined and fiery enthusiasts who followed Cromwell. They neither trusted God nor kept their powder dry.

Though the invading army entered England by way of Carlisle, Cromwell marched against them not through Lancashire but through Yorkshire. He had to supply his men with shoes and stockings from Northampton and Coventry, and to halt at Doncaster to pick up the artillery which was forwarded him from Hull, as well as to rejoin Lembert, who was in command of the small force which it had been possible to despatch to the North whilst Cromwell was detained at Pembroke, and who had been doing his best to delay the progress of the Scots till Cromwell was ready to strike home. On its march through Lancashire, Hamilton's army, some 21,000 strong, pushed slowly forward in a long straggling column, the van and the rear at too great distance from each other to be able to concentrate in case of an attack. On August 17, when Cromwell had crossed the hills into Ribblesdale and was close at hand upon his left flank, Hamilton, who had pushed on his cavalry to Wigan sixteen miles in advance, sent the bulk of his infantry across the Ribble at Preston, leaving Sir Marmaduke Langdale with 3,600 English Royalists on the north bank, whilst another detachment was some miles in the rear. It did not need much generalship to overwhelm an army under such leadership as this. Cromwell fell upon Langdale, who had posted his small force to the greatest advantage behind hedges, and after a hard tussle, carried the position and captured the greater part of the division. Then lining the steep northern bank of the Ribble with musketeers, he drove Hamilton from the flat southern bank and, later on, across the Darwen which, near this point, flows into the Ribble. What followed was little more than mere pursuit. The Scots, half starved and discouraged, were beaten wherever they attempted to make a stand, and Hamilton at last surrendered at Uttoxeter, eight days after the battle.

It was Cromwell's first victory in an independent command, and if the Scottish leader had played into his hands, he had been wanting in no part of an efficient general to profit by his folly. Once more, in the despatch in which he announced his success to the Speaker, he harped upon the old string, the duty of the Parliamentary Government to give protection to the "people of God." "Surely, Sir," he wrote, "this is nothing but the hand of God, and wherever anything in this world is exalted or exalts itself, God will put it down; for this is the day wherein He alone will be exalted. It is not fit for me to give advice, nor to say a word what use you should make of this; more than to pray you and all that acknowledge God, that they would take courage to do the work of the Lord in fulfilling the end of your magistracy in seeking the peace and welfare of this land; that all that will live peaceably may have countenance from you, and they that are incapable and will not leave troubling the land may speedily be destroyed out of the land."

On August 27, ten days after the victory at Preston, Colchester capitulated, and as far as England was concerned, the second civil war was brought to an end, only a few fortresses in the North—incapable of prolonged resistance without succour from any army in the field—still holding out. It remained to be considered what policy should be adopted towards the defeated Scots, and first of all towards the thousands of prisoners captured at Preston and in the pursuit which followed. Of these a division was made—those who had been pressed into the service being set at liberty under an engagement never again to bear arms against the Parliament of England. Those who had voluntarily taken service under Hamilton were transported to Barbados or Virginia, not, as is commonly said, as slaves, but as servants subjected for a term of years to a master who, though he usually dealt with them far more harshly than with his negro slaves, was at least bound to set them at liberty at the end of the appointed time.

The decision in this matter rested with Parliament—not with Cromwell. It was for Cromwell to follow up the relics of the Scottish army left behind to the north of Preston, and which, after the defeat of their comrades, had retreated to Scotland. Nor could it be doubted that the word of the victorious general would have great weight with Parliament in that settlement of the outstanding complaints against Scotland which was now impending. It was fortunate that this was so, as Cromwell was just the man to turn to the best advantage the dispute between the Scottish parties now bursting into a flame. The defeat of Hamilton left the way open to Argyle and that party of the more fanatical clergy whose followers in the strongly Presbyterian West were known as Whiggamores, an appellation from which the later appellation of Whig was derived. The West rose in arms, and the Whiggamore Raid—as it was called—swept from power those few partisans of Hamilton who were still at liberty, and placed Scotland once more in the hands of Argyle and the clergy. On September 21, whilst the conflict was yet undecided, Cromwell entered Scotland, demanding the surrender of Berwick and Carlisle, still occupied by Scottish garrisons. Argyle, glad of English support to strengthen his nascent authority, gave a hearty consent; and, to display the overwhelming strength of the English army to the Scottish people, Lambert was sent forward in advance, Cromwell following with the bulk of the army and arriving in Edinburgh on October 4. On the 7th Cromwell returned to England, leaving Argyle under the protection of Lambert at the head of two regiments of horse. In the meanwhile Cromwell had come to an understanding with Argyle that no Scotsman who had supported the Engagement with Charles should be allowed to retain office, a stipulation as much in accordance with Argyle's wishes as with his own. A fanatic might have objected that it was unfitting that a tolerationist should give his support to the most intolerant clergy in Protestant Europe. As a statesman, Cromwell could but remember that unless England were to assume the direct control over the Government of Scotland, it must leave such matters to local decision, especially as there were few or no Independents in Scotland to be wronged by any action which the new Government at Edinburgh might take. Yet there was undoubtedly a danger for the future in the divergency of aim between the followers of Argyle in Scotland and those of Cromwell in England.

Cromwell transferred his forces into Yorkshire to hasten the surrender of Pontefract and Scarborough, which still held out. The political interest of the day had shifted to the South. Parliament, as soon as it was relieved from danger, had determined to reopen the negotiation with the King, and the conference—known as The Treaty of Newport—commenced in the Isle of Wight on September 18. In the regiments under Cromwell's command, as well as in Fairfax's army, the disgust was intense, and Ireton now took the lead in calling for a purge of the House which would get rid of such members as supported this piece of misplaced diplomacy. To complete the dissatisfaction of the army, the demands of Parliament included the establishment of Presbyterianism without a shadow of toleration on either hand. It is unnecessary here to follow up this negotiation in detail. The objection taken to Charles's counter-proposals was less that they were themselves unjust, than that it was impossible to hinder him from slipping out of his promise whenever he felt strong enough to do so. Of this objection Ireton was the mouth-piece in Fairfax's army, and on or about November 10, he laid before the Council of officers the draft of a *Remonstrance of the Army*. It touched on many constitutional proposals, but the clause of the greatest practical interest asked "that the capital and grand author of all our troubles, the person of the King, may be speedily brought to justice for the treason, blood and mischief he is therein guilty of." The suggestion was too much for Fairfax, and he carried his officers with him in favour of a proposal that the army should ask the King to assent to the heads of a constitutional plan which would have reduced the functions of the Crown to that influence which is so beneficially exercised at the present day.

This proposal made to the King on the 16th was, however, rejected at once. The feeling of the army being what it was, Charles virtually signed his own death-warrant by this action, and it might seem to a superficial observer, as if his sufferings were due to his refusal to anticipate two centuries of history, and to abandon all the claims which had been handed down to him by his predecessors. To the careful inquirer, it is evident that the causes of the army's demand lay far deeper. The men who made it were no constitutional pedants. It was the deep distrust with which Charles had inspired them that led to this drastic mode of setting him aside from the exercise of that authority which he had so constantly abused. It was his avoidance of open and honourable speech which brought Charles to the block. Those who imagine that he was brought to the scaffold because of his refusal to submit to the abolition of episcopacy, forget that it had been in his power to secure the retention of episcopacy when it was offered him in *The Heads of the Proposals,* if only he had consented to its being accompanied by a complete toleration.

The effect of the news which Cromwell from time to time received from the army in England may be traced in the letters written by him at this time. In one which he sent to Hammond on November 6 he justified his dealings with Argyle, suggesting that the example of Scotland, where one Parliament had been dissolved and another had been elected, might be followed in England. In a second letter, written on the 20th, after he had had time to consider the rejection by Charles of the proposal of the army, he replied bitterly to an order of the House to send up Sir John Owen, a prisoner taken in Wales, that he might be banished. Cromwell angrily wrote that those who brought in the Scots had been adjudged traitors by Parliament, "this being a more prodigious treason than any that had been perfected before; because the former quarrel was that Englishmen might rule over one another, this to vassalise us to a foreign nation, and their fault who have appeared in this summer's business is certainly double theirs who were in the first, because it is the repetition of the same offence against all the witnesses that God has borne, by making and abetting a second war." "To vassalise us to a foreign nation." Here, in political matters at least, was the head and front of Charles's offending. It was this that finally broke down Cromwell's reluctance to shake himself loose from constituted authority. "God," Hammond had written, "hath appointed authorities among the nations, to which active or passive obedience is to be yielded. This resides in England in the Parliament. Therefore active or passive resistance is forbidden." To this reasoning Cromwell replied, on the 25th, by various arguments, closing with the daring suggestion that the army might, after all, be "a lawful power called by God to oppose and fight against the King upon some stated grounds; and, being in power to such ends," might not they oppose "one name of authority for these ends as well as another name?" Whatever might be the worth of these considerations, no good was to be expected from Charles. "Good," he protested, "by this man against whom the Lord hath witnessed, and whom thou knowest!"

Surely we have here laid bare before us Cromwellian opinion in the making. As in other men, the wish was father to the thought. The desire, whether for private or for public ends, shapes the thoughts, and in Cromwell's case, as the desires swept a wider compass than with most men, the thoughts took a larger scope and, to some extent, jostled with one another. The cloudy mixture would clear itself soon enough.

Meanwhile events followed quickly on one another in the south. Hammond, as too soft-hearted, was removed from Carisbrooke, and on December 1 emissaries from the army removed Charles to Hurst Castle, where he could be more easily isolated. The foremost men in the army talked openly of putting the King to death, and adopted Cromwell's suggestion that Parliament should be forcibly dissolved, and a new one elected in its place. In this sense a Declaration was issued on November 30, and on December 2 the army marched into London. The Commons showed themselves to be unaffected by threats of violence, and voted on the 5th that the King's offers were "a ground for the House to proceed upon for the settlement of the peace of the kingdom." The scheme of a dissolution favoured by the army was wrecked on the resistance of the Independent members of the House. There was to be a purge, not a dissolution followed by a general election. The plan thus agreed on was carried into practice on the morning of the 6th, when Colonel Pride stood with a military guard at the door of the House, turning back or arresting the members who had voted for a continuance of the negotiation with the King. When Cromwell returned to Westminster, on the evening of the same day, he declared that he had not "been acquainted with the design; yet, since it was done, he was glad of it, and would endeavour to maintain it." As "Pride's purge" had not been resolved on before the previous night it was physically impossible that he should have been informed of the resolution taken. There can be little doubt that he had given his sanction to the other plan of a dissolution, and had also concurred in the language ascribed to Ireton and Harrison on the previous evening. "Where," they had said of the House, "have we either law, warrant, or commission to purge it, or can anything justify us in doing it but the height of necessity to save the kingdom from a new war that they, with the conjunction of the King, will presently vote and declare for, and to procure a new and free representative, and so successive and free representatives, which this present Parliament will never suffer, and without which the freedoms of the nation are lost and gone!" It will be worth while to remember these words, when the continuance of the now truncated Parliament was at last brought to an end.

It was Cromwell's habit to accept the second best, when the best proved unattainable. As to subjecting the King to a traitor's death, Cromwell, as on so many other occasions, exercised a moderating influence. Ireton, it seems, would have been satisfied if Charles were tried and sentenced, after which he might be left in prison till he consented "to abandon his negative voice, to part from Church lands" and "to abjure the Scots." Cromwell even wanted the trial itself to be deferred. By a small majority the Army Council resolved that Charles's life should be spared. As a last effort in this direction, Lord Denbigh was despatched to Windsor—to which place Charles had been removed—to lay before him conditions on which he might yet be permitted to live. Charles, who cannot but have known the nature of the overtures now brought, refused even to see the messenger. Though no direct evidence has reached us, it can hardly be doubted that the terms offered included the renunciation of the negative voice and the abandonment of the Church, that is to say, of bishops' lands; in other words, the abandonment of control over legislation and of episcopacy. Here at last Charles found no possibility of evasion, and driven as he was to the wall, the true gold which was in him overlaid by so much ignorance and wrong-headedness revealed itself in all its purity. For him the only question was whether he should betray the ordinance of God in Church and State. The incapable ruler—the shifty intriguer—was at once revealed as the sufferer for conscience' sake.

Neither Cromwell nor his brother-officers had an inkling of this. To them Charles, in refusing this final overture, had asserted his right to be the persecutor of the godly and the obstructor of all beneficent legislation. Their patience was at length exhausted. On January 1, 1649, an ordinance was sent up to the Lords creating a High Court of Justice for the trial of the King, accompanied by a resolution that "by the fundamental laws of this kingdom it is treason in the King of England for the time being to levy war against the Parliament and Kingdom of England." "If any man whatsoever," said Cromwell when this ordinance was under debate, "hath carried on the design of deposing the King, and disinheriting his posterity; or, if any man hath yet such a design, he should be the greatest traitor and rebel in the world; but since the Providence of God hath cast this upon us, I cannot but submit to Providence, though I am not yet provided to give you advice." In the last words were the last symptoms of hesitation on Cromwell's part. Somehow or other all his efforts to save Charles from destruction had failed, and it was as much in Cromwell's nature to attribute the failure to Providence as it was in Charles's nature to regard himself as the earthly champion of the laws of God.

The House of Lords having refused to pass the ordinance, the House of Commons declared "the people to be, under God, the original of all just power," and in consequence, "the Commons of England in Parliament assembled" to be capable of giving the force of law to their enactments. From this time forth the name of an Act was given to the laws passed by a single House. On January 6, such an Act erected a High Court of Justice for the trial of the King, on the ground that he had had a wicked design to subvert his people's rights, and with this object had levied war against them, and also, having been spared, had continued to raise new commotions. Therefore, that no chief officer or magistrate might hereafter presume to contrive the enslaving or destroying of the nation, certain persons were appointed by whom Charles Stuart was to be tried.

Having once given his consent to the trial, Cromwell threw himself into the support of the resolution with all his vigour. "I tell you," he replied to some scruples of young Algernon Sidney on the score of legality, "we will cut off his head with the crown upon it." When a majority of the members of the Court refused to sit; when divisions of opinion arose amongst those who did sit; when difficulties, in short, of any kind arose, it was Cromwell who was ready with exhortation and persuasion to complete the work which they had taken in hand. His arguments appear to have been directed not to the technical point whether Charles had levied war against the nation or not, but to convince all who would listen that there had been a breach of trust in his refusal to do his utmost for the preservation of the people. Charles, on the other hand, maintained, as he was well entitled to do, that he was not being tried by any known law, and that the violence used against him would lead to the establishment of a military despotism over the land. Nothing he could say availed to change the determination of the grim masters of the hour. On January 27 sentence of death was pronounced by Bradshaw, the President of the Court, and on the 30th this sentence was carried into execution on a scaffold erected in front of the Banqueting House of his own palace of Whitehall.

That Cromwell, once his mind made up, had contributed more than any other to this result can hardly be doubted. If we are to accept a traditional story which has much to recommend it, we have something of a key to his state of mind. "The night after King Charles was beheaded," we are told, "my Lord Southhampton and a friend of his got leave to sit up by the body in the Banqueting House at Whitehall. As they were sitting very melancholy there, about two o'clock in the morning, they heard the tread of somebody coming very slowly upstairs. By-and-by the door opened, and a man entered very much muffled up in his cloak, and his face quite hid in it. He approached the body, considered it very attentively for some time, and then shook his head—sighed out the words, 'Cruel necessity!' He then departed in the same slow and concealed manner as he had come. Lord Southhampton used to say that he could not distinguish anything of his face, but that by his voice and gait he took him to be Oliver Cromwell."

Whether there was indeed any such necessity may be disputed for ever, as well as that other question whether the army had a right to force on the trial and execution in the teeth of the positive law of the land. The main issue was whether, whatever positive law might say, a king was not bound by the necessities of his position to be the representative of the nation, acting on its behalf, merging his own interests in those of his people, refusing to coerce them by foreign armies, and owing to them, whenever it became prudent to speak at all, the duty of uttering words of simple truth. So Elizabeth had acted: so Bacon had taught. That Charles's own conduct was moulded on far different principles it is impossible to deny. Confidence in his own wisdom was inherent in his nature, and there is no reason to doubt that he soberly believed his critics and antagonists to be so heated by faction that he was actually unable to do his best for the nation as well as for himself unless he called foreign armies to his aid, and raised false expectations in the hope of throwing off each party with whom he was treating, as soon as a convenient opportunity arrived. Such an attitude could not but engender resistance, and when long persisted in, necessarily called forth an attitude equally unbending. That which to Cromwell was at one time a cruel necessity—at another time a decree of Providence—was but the natural result of the offence given by Charles to men who required plain dealing in a ruler from whom nothing but ill-concealed deceitfulness was to be had. The final struggle had come to be mainly one over the King's retention of the Negative Voice, which, if he had been permitted to retain it, would enable him to hinder all new legislation which did not conform to his personal wishes. No doubt he had both law and tradition on his side, but, on the other hand, his antagonists could plead that the law of the land must depend on the resolution, not of a single person, but of the nation itself.

"Fortunately or unfortunately," I can but repeat here what

I have already said elsewhere, "such abstract considerations seldom admit of direct application to politics. It is at all times hard to discover what the wishes of a nation really are, and least of all can this be done amidst the fears and passions of a revolutionary struggle. Only after long years does a nation make clear its definite resolves, and, for this reason, wise statesmen—whether monarchical or republican—watch the currents of opinion, and submit to compromises which will enable the national sentiment to make its way without a succession of violent shocks. Charles's fault lay not so much in his claim to retain the Negative Voice, as in his absolute disregard of the conditions of the time, and of the feelings and opinions of every class of his subjects with which he happened to disagree. Even if those who opposed Charles in the later stages of his career failed to rally the majority of the people to their side, they were undoubtedly acting in accordance with a permanent national demand for that government by compromise which slowly, but irresistibly, developed itself in the course of the century.

"Nor can it be doubted that, if Charles had, under any conditions, been permitted to reseat himself on the throne, he would quickly have provoked a new resistance. As long as he remained a factor in English politics, government by compromise was impossible. His own conception of government was that of a wise prince, constantly interfering to check the madness of the people. In the Isle of Wight he wrote down with approval the lines in which Claudian, the servile poet of the Court of Honorius, declared it to be an error to give the name of slavery to the service of the best of princes, and asserted that liberty never had a greater charm than under a pious king. Even on the scaffold he reminded his subjects that a share in government was nothing appertaining to the people. It was the tragedy of Charles's life that he was utterly unable to satisfy the cravings of those who inarticulately hoped for the establishment of a monarchy which, while it kept up the old traditions of the country, and thus saved England from a blind plunge into an unknown future, would yet allow the people of the country to be to some extent masters of their own destiny.

"Yet if Charles persistently alienated this large and important section of his subjects, so also did his most determined opponents. The very merits of the Independents—their love of toleration and of legal and political reform, together with their advocacy of democratic change—raised opposition in a nation which was prepared for none of these things, and drove them step by step to rely on armed strength rather than upon the free play of constitutional action. But for this, it is probable that the Vote of No Addresses would have received a practically unanimous support in the Parliament and the nation, and that in the beginning of 1648 Charles would have been dethroned, and a new government of some kind or other established with some hope of success. As it was, in their despair of constitutional support, the Independents were led, in spite of their better feelings, to the employment of the army as an instrument of government.

"The situation, complicated enough already, had been still further complicated by Charles's duplicity. Men who would have been willing to come to terms with him despaired of any constitutional arrangement in which he was to be a factor, and men who had been long alienated from him were irritated into active hostility. By these he was regarded with increasing intensity as the one disturbing force with which no understanding was possible and no settled order consistent. To remove him out of the way appeared, even to those who had no thought of punishing him for past offences, to be the only possible road to peace for the troubled nation. It seemed that, so long as Charles lived, deluded nations and deluded parties would be stirred up by promises never intended to be fulfilled, to fling themselves, as they had flung themselves in the Second Civil War, against the new order of things which was struggling to establish itself in England.

"Of this latter class Cromwell made himself the mouthpiece. Himself a man of compromises, he had been thrust, sorely against his will, into direct antagonism with the uncompromising King. He had striven long to mediate between the old order and the new, first by restoring Charles as a constitutional King, and afterwards by substituting one of his children for him. Failing in this, and angered by the persistence with which

Charles stirred up Scottish armies and Irish armies against England, Cromwell finally associated himself with those who cried out most loudly for the King's blood. No one knew better than Cromwell that it was folly to cover the execution of the King with the semblance of constitutional propriety, and he may well have thought that, though law and constitution had both broken down, the first step to be taken towards their reconstruction was the infliction of the penalty of death upon the man who had shown himself so wanting in the elementary quality of veracity upon which laws and constitutions are built up. All that is known of Cromwell's conduct at the trial points to his contempt for the legal forms with which others were attempting to cover an action essentially illegal."

A further question which has been often mooted is whether Cromwell—whatever may be said on the purity of his motives—did not commit a blunder in respect of the interests of himself and his cause. If those who have discussed this problem mean that the attempt to establish a free government during Cromwell's lifetime was rendered more difficult by the execution of the King, it is hard to gainsay their opinion, though the estrangement of the bulk of the population from the new order, in consequence of the execution, is probably very much exaggerated. Those who, like the Cavaliers, had been mulcted of a portion of their estates had an additional reason for detesting a government which had used them so ill, and there must have been a certain number amongst the crowds who read the *Eikon Basilike*—the little book in which Charles's vindication of his life was supposed to have been written by his own hand—who were permanently affected by that sentimental production of Dr. Gauden. If, however, it is argued that Cromwell and his allies might possibly have succeeded in establishing a government to their taste if they had abstained from inflicting the last penalty on the King, it can only be answered that other causes made their success in the highest degree improbable. Their plans for the benefit of the people were on the one hand too far advanced to secure popular support; and, on the other hand, too defective in fair-play to their opponents to deserve it. Puritanism was not, and never could be the national religion, and though it made more enemies through its virtues than through its defects, those who strove to enforce its moral and social precepts needed a strong military force at their backs. The irritation caused by the interference of the army in religion and politics, and by the demands on the tax-payer which the maintenance of the army rendered necessary, would surely have been fatal to any government resting on such a basis, even if Charles had been suffered to prolong his days. If there remains any interest in Cromwell's career after the execution of the King it arises from his constantly renewed efforts to throw off this incubus, and his repeated failures to achieve his purpose.

Chapter 4

The Last Years of the Long Parliament

DURING THE LAST WEEKS of Charles's life, the army, in co-operation with some of the Levellers, had drawn up an enlarged edition of *The Agreement of the People,* a task which was completed on January 15. In accordance with Cromwell's wish, this proposed constitution was laid before Parliament on the 20th for its approval, instead of being imposed on Parliament by a previous vote amongst the so-called well affected. Parliament being sufficiently busy at the time, laid the proposal aside with a few well-chosen compliments. The members had no wish to engage, at such a moment, in the uncertainties of a general election.

There can be little doubt that in this matter Parliament was instinctively in the right. That mutilated Assembly to which modern writers give the name of "the Rump," though no such word was employed by contemporaries till its reappearance on the scene some time after Cromwell's death, was in possession of the field. It now contented itself with proclaiming England to be a Commonwealth without King or House of Lords, and with electing an annually renewable Council of State to perform executive functions under its own control. The first political act of the sovereign Parliament was to order the execution of the Duke of Hamilton, the Earl of Holland, and Lord Capel, who, having taken the King's part in the last war, had been condemned by a High

Court of Justice, similar to the one that had sent Charles to the block. For the moment the most serious danger to the young Commonwealth arose from the opposition of Lilburne and the Levellers, who, not content with asking, on the ground of abstract principles, for the immediate foundation of a democratic Republic in the place of the existing make-shift arrangement, extended their propaganda to the army itself, appealing to the private soldiers against the officers. Lilburne and three of his supporters were summoned before the Council. Lilburne, having threatened to burn down any place in which he might be imprisoned, was directed to retire. From the outer room he listened to the voices in the Council chamber. "I tell you, sir," said Cromwell, "you have no other way of dealing with these men but to break them, or they will break you; yea, and bring all the guilt of the blood and treasure shed and spent in this kingdom upon your heads and shoulders; and frustrate and make void all that work that, with so many years' industry, toil and pains you have done, and so render you to all rational men in the world as the most contemptiblest generation of silly, low-spirited men in the earth, to be broken and routed by such a despicable, contemptible generation of men as they are, and therefore, Sir, I tell you again, you are necessitated to break them." We can sympathise with Lilburne now in his desire to establish government by the people, to confirm individual right, and to restrain the commanders of the army from political power. Yet, after all, the practical necessities of the hour were on Cromwell's side.

It was not long before the mutinous spirit to which Lilburne appealed showed itself in the army. A regiment quartered at Salisbury refused obedience to its officers, and roamed about the country seeking for other bodies of troops with which to combine. Fairfax set out from London in chase, and on the night of May 14 Cromwell, by a forced march with his cavalry, overtook the mutineers at Burford. Three were executed, and the remainder submitted to the inevitable.

It was the more necessary to keep the army in hand, as there was renewed fighting in prospect. The eldest son of the late King, now claiming the title of Charles II, was about to make an effort to seat himself on his father's throne, and hoped, as his father had hoped before him, to have on his side the forces of Scotland and Ireland. For many years the problem of the relations between the three countries had been inviting a solution. Both Scotland and Ireland had social and political interests of their own, and the natural reluctance of the inhabitants of either country to see these merged in those of the wealthier and more numerous people of England would in any case have called for delicate handling. The rise for the first time of a powerful army in England made her relations with the two other countries even more difficult than before, and had contributed fully as much as zeal for Presbyterianism to the ridiculous scheme of re-establishing Charles I as a covenanting King. After the defeat of Hamilton, indeed, Argyle and the Scottish clergy had welcomed Cromwell's support in the overthrow of the power of the nobility, but the dread of English predominance had not been entirely dispelled, and the King's execution added a sentimental grievance to other causes of alarm. In refusing to allow any English government to dispose of Scotland, the Scots were undoubtedly within their rights; but when on February 5 they proclaimed Charles II not merely as King of Scotland, but as King of Great Britain, France and Ireland, they took up a position which no English government could allow to remain unchallenged, whilst in adding a condition that Charles was to be admitted to power only on his engagement to rule according to the National Covenant and the Solemn League and Covenant, they put forward the monstrous claim to control the religious development of England and Ireland, as well as of their own country.

The necessity—according to these conditions—of coming to an understanding with Charles, made Scotland little dangerous for the moment, and enabled the English Parliament to turn its attention to Ireland, to which Charles I had looked hopefully after the failure of the Hamilton invasion. Ormond, who had formerly headed Charles's partisans in Ireland, now returned to that country as the King's Lord Lieutenant, and brought under his leadership, not only his old followers, but the army of the Confederate Catholics. Though Owen O'Neill, at the head of an army raised amongst the Celts of Ulster, kept aloof, the way seemed open for Ormond to attack Dublin, which was now guarded by a Parliamentary garrison under Michael Jones, and was almost the only place in Ireland still holding out for England. As in Scotland, so in Ireland, the question was not so much whether England was to win forcible mastery over those portions of the British Isles outside her borders, as whether they were to be used to determine the political institutions of England herself. The attacks on Ireland and Scotland, which were now to follow, were in a certain sense acts of defensive warfare.

To no man more than Cromwell was this thought present. An Englishman of Englishmen—his bitterest complaint against the late King had been that he had attempted to "vassalise" England to a foreign nation, and when on March 15 he was named to the command, he explained to his brother officers the reasons which inclined him to accept the post. "Truly," he said, "this is really believed:—If we do not endeavour to make good our interest there, and that timely, we shall not only have our interest rooted out there, but they will, in a very short time, be able to land forces in England and put us to trouble here; and I confess I have these thoughts with myself that perhaps may be carnal and foolish: I had rather be overrun with a Cavalierish interest than a Scottish interest; had rather be overrun by a Scottish interest than an Irish interest, and I think of all this is most dangerous; and, if they shall be able to carry on their work, they will make this the most miserable people in the earth; for all the world knows their barbarism—not of any religion almost any of them, but, in a manner, as bad as Papists—and truly it is thus far that the quarrel is brought to this State that we can hardly return into that tyranny that formerly we were under the yoke of . . . but we must at the same time be subject to the kingdom of Scotland and the kingdom of Ireland for the bringing in of the King. Now it should awaken all Englishmen who perhaps are willing enough he should have come in upon an accommodation; but now he must come in from Ireland or Scotland."

In these words are revealed the convictions that dominated Cromwell's action at this period of his life. So far as it lay in him, he would never admit that Scotland, still less that Ireland, should impose a government upon England. On July 12 he set out for Ireland. Before he could embark he received the welcome news that Michael Jones had defeated Ormond at Rathmines, and that Dublin was consequently out of danger. When he landed at Dublin, his intention was, as soon as possible, to make his way into Munster and rally round him the Protestant colonists who formed a considerable part of the population of the towns on the coast. It was, however, necessary first to protect Dublin from an attack from the north, from which quarter Owen O'Neill, who, after long hesitation, had thrown in his lot with Ormond, was expected to advance. Accordingly, on September 1, Cromwell marched upon Drogheda, which was held for the King by a garrison of about 2,800 men, mainly composed of Irishmen, under Sir Arthur Aston. On the 10th Cromwell summoned the place, and on the refusal of the governor to surrender opened a cannonade on the south-eastern angle. It was impossible for the garrison—short of ammunition as it was—to hold out long, and on the second day, when a breach had been effected, Cromwell gave the word to storm. The assailants, though twice driven back, were, on the third attempt, successful. Aston, with about three hundred men, took refuge on a huge artificial mound, known as the Mill Mount. Angry at the prolonged resistance, Cromwell gave the word to put to the sword all who were in arms. The hasty word was ruthlessly obeyed, and some two thousand men were slaughtered in cold blood. There is no doubt that in what he did, Cromwell was covered by the strict law of war, which placed a garrison refusing surrender outside the pale of mercy; but the law had seldom been acted on in the English war, and it is permissible to doubt whether Cromwell would have acted on it on this occasion, if the defenders had been other than "Irish Papists," as he scornfully called them. The memory of the Ulster massacre of 1641, not merely as it really was, but accompanied by all the exaggerations to which it had been subjected by English rumour, was ever present to his mind, and he regarded every Irishman in arms, not as an honourable antagonist, but as either a murderer or a supporter of murderers.

Yet even Cromwell seems to have thought the deed deserving of excuse. "Truly," he wrote to Bradshaw, the President of the Council, "I believe this bitterness will save much effusion of blood through the goodness of God. I wish that all honest hearts may give the glory of this to God alone, to whom indeed the praise of this mercy belongs." "I am persuaded," he assured Lenthall, "that this is a righteous judgment of God upon those barbarous wretches who have imbrued their hands in so much innocent blood, and it will tend to prevent the effusion of blood for the future, which are the satisfactory grounds for such actions, which otherwise cannot but work remorse or regret."

Leaving a garrison behind him in Drogheda, Cromwell marched to the south by way of Wexford. There too a slaughter took place, though this time it was brought on by the act of the townsmen, who continued their resistance after the walls had been scaled. The story often repeated of the two or three hundred women killed in the market place is pure fiction, of which nothing is heard till after the middle of the eighteenth century. On the other hand, both at Drogheda and Wexford priests were put to death without mercy. Whether these cruelties, in the long run, rendered Irishmen more ready to submit to the invaders may be doubted, but they certainly made Cromwell's path easier whilst the terror spread by them was recent. Wexford fell on October 11. On the 17th Cromwell summoned New Ross. "I have this witness for myself," he wrote to the Governor, "that I have endeavoured to avoid effusion of blood—this being my principle that the people and the places where I come may not suffer except through their own wilfulness." Two days later he was asked whether he would grant liberty of conscience. "I meddle not," he answered, "with any man's conscience, but if by liberty of conscience, you mean liberty to exercise the mass, I judge it best to use plain dealing, and to let you know that where the Parliament of England have power that will not be allowed of." Cromwell's principle in Ireland was very much what Elizabeth's had been in England. Men might hold what religious opinions they pleased, but toleration was not to be extended to the Roman Catholic worship. The distinction may appear unjustifiable in the eyes of the present generation. It was perfectly familiar to the statesmen of the seventeenth century.

Before long Cromwell's hope of support from the Protestants in the south was amply justified. Cork was the first of the coast towns in Munster to rise in his favour, and others soon followed the example. Waterford, on the other hand, held out, being assisted by the winter rains. The first months of 1650 were employed in the reduction of towns further inland, such as Kilkenny and Clonmel, though the garrison of the latter place succeeded in making its escape. After the surrender of Clonmel Cromwell left Ireland, his services being required at home. Ireton, who remained behind as Lord Deputy, had nearly completed the conquest when he died in November 1651 of a disease caused by his devotion to the calls of duty, though the last fortified post did not surrender till April 1653.

Cromwell's reason for treating the Irish Roman Catholics with peculiar harshness may be gathered from a controversy in which he took part some time before he left the country. In December 1649 the Irish Prelates assembled at Clonmacnoise issued a Declaration in which they warned their flocks that Cromwell was bent on extirpating the Catholic religion, and could not effect his purpose "without the massacring or banishment of the Catholic inhabitants." They proceeded to point out that those who were spared by the sword were doomed to impoverishment, as by English Acts of Parliament already passed, "the estates of the inhabitants of this kingdom are sold, so there remaineth now no more but to put the purchasers in possession by the power of forces drawn out of England, and for the common sort of people, to whom they show any more moderate usage at present, it is to no other end but for their private advantage, and for the better support of their army, intending at the close of their conquest, if they can effect the same—as God forbid—to root out the commons also, and plant this land with colonies to be brought hither out of England—as witness the number they have already sent hence for the Tobacco Islands—and put enemies in their place." The Prelates concluded by declaring that, henceforth, clergy and laity would unite to defend the Church, the King and the nation.

In one part of this declaration the Prelates had referred to the English army as "the common enemy." "Who is it," asked Cromwell wrathfully in reply, "that created this common enemy? I suppose you mean Englishmen. The English! Remember, ye hypocrites, Ireland was once united to England; Englishmen had good inheritances, which many of them purchased with their money, they or their ancestors, from many of you and your ancestors. They had good leases from Irishmen for long time to come, great stocks thereupon, houses and plantations erected at their cost and charge. They lived peaceably and honestly amongst you; you had generally equal benefit of the protection of England with them, and equal justice from the laws—saving what was necessary for the State, upon reasons of State, to put upon some few people apt to rebel upon the instigation of such as you. You broke the union; you unprovoked put the English to the most unheard of and most barbarous massacre without respect of sex or age that ever the sun beheld, and at a time when Ireland was at perfect peace, and when, through the example of English industry, through commerce and traffic, that which was in the natives' hands was better to them than if all Ireland had been in their possession and not an Englishman in it; and yet then, I say, was this unheard of villainy perpetrated through your instigation, who boast of peace-making and union against the common enemy. What think you, by this time? Is not my assertion true? Is God—will God be with you? I am confident He will not."

Such was the picture which framed itself in Cromwell's mind in the contemplation of the troubles of 1641. It was no long by-past history that he ignored—though the race against which his sword was drawn was one singularly retentive of the tradition of days long-ago. It was the occurrences which had passed in his own life-time which he misinterpreted. The Irish peoples and tribes, it seemed, had had no grievances of which to complain. They had never, forsooth, been ousted from their land by the chicanery of English lawyers and English statesmen. As for their religion, it was hardly to be regarded as a religion at all. Favour enough was shown to them if they were allowed to bury their creed in their hearts, though they were deprived of those consolations on which those who held their faith were far more dependent than the adherents of other Churches. That Cromwell believed every word he said is not to be doubted. This representation of Irish problems and of Irish facts was no creation of his own mind. It was the common—probably the universal belief of Englishmen of his own day.

Nor was Cromwell any more original in propounding remedies. "We are come," he continued, "to take an account of the innocent blood that hath been shed, and to endeavour to bring them to account—by the blessing of Almighty God, in whom alone is our hope and strength—who by appearing in arms seek to justify the same. We come to break the power of a company of lawless rebels who, having cast off the authority of England, live as enemies to human society, whose principles—the world hath experience of—are to destroy and subjugate all men not complying with them. We come—by the assistance of God—to hold forth and maintain the lustre and glory of English liberty, in a nation where we have an undoubted right to do it, whereas the people of Ireland—if they listen not to such seducers as you are—may equally participate in all benefits to use liberty and fortune equally with Englishmen, if they keep out of arms." Irishmen, in short, were to be what Englishmen were, or to bear the penalty. It was the old remedy of the Elizabethans and of Strafford. It is not so much the victorious sword that alienates as the contempt of the conqueror for all that the conquered are in themselves or for all that they hold dear. Yet it must be acknowledged that in whatever proportion the guilt of past errors may be divisible between English and Irish, no English government could endure longer to face that danger of invasion from the side of Ireland, which had so constantly threatened England since first her civil broils began. Under these circumstances, an English conquest of Ireland was inevitable as soon as it was undertaken by a disciplined army. Irishmen were too deeply riven asunder by diversities of race and institutions to unite in common resistance; and even if these difficulties could be removed, there was no common leader who commanded universal devotion. Conquered—Ireland was bound to be, but it was unfortunate for both peoples that she was conquered at a time when the religious and political ideas of Englishmen were, more than ever before or since, the antithesis of those of Irishmen. It was when a Puritan Government took in hand what they hoped to be the regeneration of Ireland that the real difficulties of the task would be made manifest.

No such gulf was open between England and Scotland, yet the apprehension of fresh troubles approaching from Scotland caused the Government at Westminster to recall Cromwell in May 1650. For some time a negotiation had been carried on at Breda between the exiled Charles II and a body of commissioners who had been sent by the extreme Presbyterians now dominant in Edinburgh, with the object of persuading the young King to accept their assistance to regain his other kingdoms on conditions which could not fail to be most repulsive to him. He was to disallow the treaty concluded by Ormond, by which the Irish were exempted from the penal laws, though in that treaty lay his sole hope of resisting Cromwell in that country; he was to establish Presbyterianism both in England and Ireland without a shred of toleration either for the sects or for that Church of which he was himself a member, and he was to sign the two Covenants, marking his own adhesion to the Scottish form of religion. Against these terms Charles long struggled, but on May 1 he signed the draft of an agreement assenting to them, which was sent to Scotland for approval, accompanied by a demand on his part for their modification. Before an answer was received, Charles heard that his most gallant champion, Montrose, had been defeated and hanged as a traitor. A day or two later, on June 1, he was informed that his request for the modification of the Scottish terms had been rejected at Edinburgh. On the 2nd Charles embarked for Scotland without signing anything, and it was only on June 11, off

Heligoland, that he affixed his name to the treaty, and only on the 23rd, off Speymouth, that he swore to the Covenants, as the treaty required him to do. There can be little doubt that he intended to cast off the bondage as soon as an opportunity arrived. It is doubtful which was the greater, the ignorance of the Scottish Government in supposing that their conditions could be imposed on England, or their folly in imagining that Charles would be bound by his oath to become their accomplice. Of this Government Argyle was still the leading personality, but that shrewd statesman only held his own by submitting to the crowd of fanatics, clerical and lay, whom he had once hoped to control, and who now made themselves his masters. Secret communications had long been passing between Charles and his English supporters. They were expected to rise in support of the Scots, but as to the engagement to establish Presbyterianism, it "was by most refused, and resolved to be broken by those who took it."

Under these circumstances, Cromwell's return had been ardently expected by all who had attached themselves to the existing Government. Whilst he was still absent, Parliament had secured to him the use of the Cockpit—a house opposite Whitehall—and also of St. James's House and Spring Gardens; and had afterwards voted to him an additional grant of lands bringing in £2,500 a year. On June 1 he had a magnificent reception as he crossed Hounslow Heath, and on the 4th received the thanks of Parliament for his services. The first question mooted was on whom should be bestowed the command of the army destined for the north. As long as it was expected that the troops were to act on the defensive, Fairfax was ready to go with Cromwell serving under him, as in old days, as his Lieutenant-General.

On June 20, when it was resolved, doubtless at Cromwell's suggestion, that the English army should invade Scotland to anticipate an attack which was regarded as inevitable, Fairfax's hesitations began, and after a brief delay he offered to resign his commission. Cromwell did his best to combat his arguments, which proceeded rather from a general feeling of distrust of the tendency of the Commonwealth Government than from any distinct resolve to separate himself from it.

Cromwell's persuasions were of no avail, and on June 26 he received the appointment of Lord General, which Fairfax was now permitted to resign. Cromwell's mind was set on something more than military success. In a conversation with Ludlow, who was about to leave for Ireland, he discoursed for an hour on the 110 Psalm. "He looked," he said, "on the design of the Lord in this day to be the freeing of the people from every burden." Especially he found hard words to fling at the lawyers—those sons of Zeruiah who had hitherto stood in the way of the simplifying of the law in favour of poorer litigants.

On June 28 Cromwell set out for his command. At Berwick on July 19 he found himself at the head of 16,000 men, whilst the Scottish army, under the command of David Leslie, numbered 26,000. For the first time in his life Cromwell was opposed to a general who was a capable strategist. The Scottish army, moreover, had the advantage of position. Occupying Edinburgh Castle and the fortified city sloping eastwards beneath it, Leslie had thrown up intrenchments from the foot of the Canongate to Leith, to bar the way to any army threatening to cut off the city from its port. Cromwell, having failed to carry this line, retreated to Musselburgh to prepare for his next step.

Though the Scots had the advantage of military position, their army had none of the coherence of the English. The clergy, under whose influence it had been gathered, had a shrewd suspicion that Charles was not whole-hearted in his devotion to the Kirk. They were afraid of his influence on the soldiers, and when he made his appearance at Leith they compelled him to withdraw. His expulsion was followed by a purge of the army, and in three days no fewer than 80 officers and 3,000 soldiers were dismissed as not coming up to the proper spiritual or moral standard. To the clergy Cromwell's appeal was directed in vain. "I beseech you," he wrote to them, "in the bowels of Christ, think it possible you may be mistaken." It was the very last thing they were prepared to do. To them sectarianism was an evil to be combated at all hazards, and Cromwell's entreaties to join him in brotherly union met with no response. Yet amongst the stricter Presbyterian laity there were some—such as Strachan and Ker—who felt uncomfortable at being told that they were fighting for a malignant King. Cromwell having posted himself, on August 13, on Braid Hill, to the south of Edinburgh, committed one of the greatest faults of which a general is capable. His eagerness to win over those whom—in spite of their contumelious rejection of his claim—he persisted in regarding as his brothers in religion, led him to subordinate war to diplomacy. For the first time in his military career he was hesitating and tentative, prone to delay action, and above all inspired by the hope that action might be avoided. Even if he had acted more promptly it is possible that he might have failed against so wary an antagonist as Leslie. His plan, probably the best under the circumstances, was to march on Queensferry, in order to cut the communications of the Scottish army with its base of supplies in Fife, communications which could not be maintained lower down the Firth where the English fleet was master of the sea. Leslie held the inner line, and when at last, on August 27, Cromwell advanced towards Queensferry, he found Leslie across his path, posted behind a morass. He could but turn back once more to Musselburgh, after which, giving up the game he had been playing for some weeks, he found himself, on September 1, at Dunbar. Leslie followed, taking care to avoid a battle and drawing up his army on Doon Hill, whose steep slopes looked down on the flatter ground on which Cromwell's forces lay. Blocking the route to England by occupying the defile at Cockburnspath, Leslie had but to remain where he was to force Cromwell—now commanding less than half his former numbers—either to surrender or to ship the best part of his force for England—the fleet which accompanied him not affording space for the accommodation of his whole army. "The enemy," wrote Cromwell, "lieth so upon the hills that we know not how to come that way without difficulty, and our lying here daily consumeth our men who fall sick beyond imagination." There could be little doubt that even if the army secured its retreat to its own country, its failure to defeat the Scots would be followed by a general rising of the Cavaliers in England.

Humanly speaking, the prospect was a dark one, and Cromwell could but console himself with his trust in Divine assistance. "All," he wrote, "shall work for good; our spirits are comfortable, praised be the Lord, though our present condition be as it is, and indeed we have much hope in the Lord, of Whose mercy we have had large experience." With him faith in Divine protection was consistent with the adoption of every military measure by which an adversary's mistakes could be turned to his own advantage. It was otherwise with the clergy and their adherents, who exercised so much influence on the Doon Hill. There had been fresh purging of the Scottish army, and soldiers had again been dismissed—not for any lack of military efficiency, but because their views of the Covenant were insufficiently exalted. It is said that the men who were thus weakening their own fighting power grew impatient with Leslie for not crushing the enemy by an immediate onslaught. Other causes may have combined to make the postponement of a conflict almost impossible. There was no water on the Doon Hill, and provisions for 23,000 men must have been hard to come by in that bleak region. At all events, on the 2nd the Scots began to move down the Hill. The struggle was to be transformed from a competition in strategy to a competition in tactics, and Cromwell, sure of mastery in that field, was rejoiced at the sight which met his eyes. In the early morning of the 3rd a plan of action brilliantly conceived was skilfully carried into execution; and the Scots, after a brave resistance, broke and fled. As the sun rose out of the sea, Cromwell, with the joyful exclamation on his lips: "Let God arise, let His enemies be scattered," pushed his victorious cavalry in pursuit. Before they drew rein, 3,000 of the enemy had been slain, and 10,000 captured together with the whole of the artillery. Never again did a Scottish army take the field to impose its religion upon a recalcitrant England.

"Surely," wrote Cromwell, after the battle had been won, "it's probable the Kirk has done their do. I believe their King will set up upon his own score now, wherein he will find many friends." Charles himself seems to have taken the same view of the situation if it be true that, on receiving the news from Dunbar, he gave thanks to God "that he was so fairly rid of his enemies." At all events the key to the history of the next twelve months in Scotland is the attempt to convert a clerical into a national resistance. To Cromwell, an attempt to force England into political conformity with Scotland was as much to be resisted as an attempt to impose on her the Scottish religion. It was the despotic tendencies, not the fervour of that religion, that he disliked. The association of the laity with the clergy in the government of the Church was insufficient for him. His ideal community was one in which every layman was capable of performing spiritual functions. He would not listen to the objection of a colonel who complained that one of his officers "was a better preacher than fighter." "Truly," he replied, "I think that he that prays and preaches best, will fight best. I know nothing will give like courage as the knowledge of God in Christ will, and I bless God to see any in this army able and willing to impart the knowledge they have, for the good of others; and I expect it be encouraged by all the chief officers in this army especially; and I hope you will do so. I pray receive Captain Empson lovingly; I dare assure you he is a good man and a good officer. I would we had no worse."

Unluckily there was no response amongst the Scottish laymen to such an appeal as this. They were satisfied—if religiously inclined—with the part assigned to them on Kirk Sessions or Presbyteries, and preferred to take their sermons from an ordained minister. Even those Presbyterians who distrusted a malignant King held aloof from the sectarian Englishman.

In England, the news of the great victory was enthusiastically received. One hundred and sixty Scottish flags were hung up in Westminster Hall, and Parliament ordered that a medal, known as the "Dunbar Medal," the first war medal granted to an English army, should bear Cromwell's likeness on one side. Against this glorifying of himself Cromwell protested in vain, but for all that he could say, his own lineaments were not excluded. His work in Scotland was however far from being accomplished. The victory of Dunbar was in time followed by the surrender of Edinburgh Castle, brought about, it is said, by the treachery of the governor; but it was in vain that the conqueror attempted to win over the extreme Covenanters who held out in the west under Strachan and Ker, and in the end he had to send Lambert against them. Lambert fell upon them at Hamilton and broke their power of resistance.

In the meantime, the tendency to resist the pretensions of the clergy was slowly making its way. On January 1, 1651, Charles was duly crowned at Scone, swearing not only to approve of the Covenants in Scotland, but to give his Royal assent to acts and ordinances of Parliament, passed and to be passed, enjoining the same in his other dominions. The young King protested his sincerity and begged the Ministers present to show him so much favour as "that if in any time coming they did hear or see him breaking that Covenant, they would tell him of it, and put him in mind of his oath." For all that, Charles was busily undermining the party of the Covenant. One by one of the leaders of the Hamilton party—Hamilton himself—a brother of the Duke who had been beheaded at Westminster,—and who, when still only Earl of Lanark, had been deeply concerned in patching up the Engagement with Charles I—Middleton, the rough soldier who had fought Charles I, and Lauderdale, the ablest of those Presbyterians who had rallied to the throne, were admitted, after humbly acknowledging their offences to the Kirk, to take their seats in Parliament, and to place their swords at the King's disposal. Argyle, who had triumphed over these men in his prosperity, was driven to seek refuge in his Highland home at Inverary. His policy of heading a democratic party organised by the clergy had fallen to the ground without hope of recovery. The national movement had passed into the hands of the nobility.

In the spring and early summer of 1651 Cromwell had thus to face a resistance based on a national policy rather than on extreme Covenanting grounds. For the present he had to leave his enemies unassailed. He was lying at Edinburgh, stricken down by illness, and for some time his life was despaired of. More than ever, indeed, he had the strength of England to fall back on. Englishmen had no desire to submit to Scottish dictation. Conspiracies for a Royalist insurrection were firmly suppressed, and suspected Royalists committed to prison as a preventive measure. At the same time a body of the new militia, which had been recently organised, was entrusted to Harrison—the fierce enthusiast who had been left in charge of the forces remaining in England, and who was now directed to guard the northern border against the Scottish invasion.

At last Cromwell was himself again. In the first days of June Charles's new army lay at Stirling. The seizure and imprisonment of his English partisans had deprived him of all hope of raising a diversion in the south, and Leslie was compelled to fall back on the defensive tactics by which he had guarded Edinburgh the year before. During the first fortnight of July Cromwell laboured in vain to bring on an engagement. Leslie, strongly posted amongst the hills to the south of Stirling, was not to be induced to repeat the error he had committed at Dunbar, and this time provisions and water could be obtained without difficulty. If Cromwell did not intend to waste his army away, he must transfer it to the enemy's rear, with a certain result of leaving the road open for their advance into England. Six months before, whilst the chiefs of English royalism were still at large, it would have been a most hazardous plan. Now that they were under arrest, it might be attempted with impunity. Lambert was sent across to North Queensferry, and on July 20 he defeated, at Inverkeithing, a Scottish force sent out from Stirling against him. Before long Cromwell followed his lieutenant, and on August 2 Perth fell into his hands. The communications of the Scottish army at Stirling were thus cut, and there was nothing before it but to march southwards on the uncertain prospect of being still able to find allies in England. That Cromwell had been able to accomplish this feat was owing partly to his command of the sea, which had enabled him with safety to send Lambert across the Forth, partly to his knowledge that the materials of the Scottish army were far inferior to those of his own. Had Leslie been at the head of a force capable of meeting the invaders in the field, Cromwell at Perth might indeed have found himself in an awkward position, as, in case of defeat, he might easily have been driven back to perish in the Highlands. On the other hand, it must be acknowledged that the English General had been learning from his opponent. It was now—unless the campaign of Preston be excepted, when his march upon Hamilton's flank had been decided by the necessity of picking up his artillery in Yorkshire—that Cromwell, for the first time in his life, developed strategical power, that is to say, the power of combining movements, the result of which would place the enemy in a false position. Already, before he followed Lambert, he had summoned Harrison to Linlithgow, and had ordered him to keep the Scots in check as they marched through England.

The first rumour that the Scottish army had broken up from Stirling and was on its way to the south reached Cromwell on August 1. On the 2nd, leaving 6,000 men under Monk—a soldier well tried in the Irish wars—to complete the subjugation, he started in pursuit. "The enemy," he wrote to Lenthall, "in his desperation and fear, and out of inevitable necessity, is run to try what he can do this way." Cromwell was never less taken by surprise. "I do apprehend," he continued, "that if he goes for England, being some few days' march before us, it will trouble some men's thoughts, and may occasion some men's inconveniences, of which I hope we are as deeply sensible, and have been, and I trust shall be as diligent to prevent as any. And indeed this is our comfort that in simplicity of heart as towards God we have done to the best of our judgments, knowing that if some issue were not put to this business it would occasion another winter's war to the ruin of your soldiery, for whom the Scots are too hard in respect of enduring the winter difficulties of this country, and would have been under the endless expense of the treasure of England in prosecuting this war. It may be supposed we might have kept the enemy from this by interposing between him and England, which truly I believe we might; but how to remove him out of this place without doing what we have done, unless we had a commanding army on both sides of the river of Forth, is not clear to us; or how to answer the inconveniences above mentioned we understand not. We pray, therefore, that—seeing there is a probability for the enemy to put you to some trouble—you would, with the same courage grounded upon a confidence in God, wherein you have been supported to the great things God hath used you in hitherto, improve, the best you can, such forces as you have in readiness as may on the sudden be gathered together to give the enemy some check until we shall be able to reach up to him, which we trust in the Lord we shall do our utmost endeavour in."

Instructions were despatched to Harrison to attend the enemy's march upon his flanks whilst Lambert hung upon his rear as he moved by way of Carlisle and Lancaster. Cromwell himself pushed on by the eastern route to head off the Scots as soon as he could gain sufficiently upon their slower march. The only question of importance was to know which of the opposing armies could gain most assistance in England. In Lancashire indeed the Earl of Derby raised a force for the King, but he was defeated by Robert Lilburne at Wigan, and was himself captured. When on August 22 Charles reached Worcester, scarcely a single Englishman had joined him. Large bodies of militia, on the other hand, flocked to Cromwell's standard; and when on September 3—the anniversary of Dunbar—the final battle was fought at Worcester, Cromwell commanded some 31,000 men, whilst the Scottish army did not number above 16,000. Cromwell having laid bridges of boats across the Severn and the Teme, was able to shift his regiments from one bank to the other of either stream as occasion served, and the Scots, fighting their best, were crushed by superior numbers as well as by superior discipline. Charles, when all was lost, rode away from the place of slaughter, and after an adventurous journey, made his escape to France. "The dimensions of this mercy," wrote Cromwell, "are above my thoughts. It is, for aught I know, a crowning mercy. Surely if it be not, such a one we shall have, if this provoke those that are concerned in it to thankfulness, and the Parliament to do the will of Him who hath done His will for it and for the nation, whose good pleasure it is to establish the nation and the change of government, by making the people so willing to the defence thereof, and so signally blessing the endeavours of your servants in this great work."

Was it really in defence of "the change of government" that the people had sided with Cromwell? Or was it merely that they would not tolerate a Scottish conquest? At all events, the tide of feeling gave to the Parliament a momentary strength. Of the notable Scots engaged, Hamilton had fallen at Worcester, and the greater number of the remainder were now consigned to English prisons. Of the few Englishmen who had risen, Derby was beheaded at Bolton-le-Moors, four of his followers being subsequently executed. The subjugation of Scotland was completed by Monk.

As for Cromwell, he settled down into a quiet and unpretentious life, attending to the discipline of the army, and ready in his place in Parliament to forward the cause which he had most at heart—the establishment of that Commonwealth to which his victories had given a breathing-space. To him, as to many disinterested observers, the time had come to found the government no longer on the sword, but on the consent of the nation, and there can be little doubt that at no time between 1642 and 1660 was there more chance of gaining a majority for the new system than this. Cromwell, at least, did everything in his power to procure a vote for an early dissolution. It was only, however, by a majority of two that Parliament agreed to fix a date for its dissolution, following the vote by a resolution postponing that event for three years. There can be little doubt that this resolution found support amongst those members who were fattening on corruption; but there was also something to be said for the view taken some time before by Marten, when he compared the Commonwealth to Moses, because the members now sitting "were the true mother to this fair child, the young Commonwealth," and therefore its fittest nurses. A general election is always somewhat of a lottery, and it was the weakest part of the system—or want of system—on which the Commonwealth was based, that it never represented the people as a whole, and that its actions might easily have been repudiated by them if they had been consulted.

Baffled in his desire to secure an immediate appeal to the electors, Cromwell prepared to use the time which the members had secured for themselves, by coming to an understanding with the leading statesmen on the principles of the future Government. He had never committed himself to the doctrine that the executive authority ought to be placed directly in the hands of an elected assembly or of a council subordinated to it. When at the conference now held the lawyers pleaded that Charles II or the Duke of York might be called on to accept the government if the rights of Englishmen could be safeguarded, he replied somewhat oracularly: "That will be a business of more than ordinary difficulty; but really, I think, if it may be done with safety and preservation of our rights as Englishmen and Christians, that a settlement with somewhat of a monarchical power in it would be very effectual." It is very unlikely that Cromwell, being what he was, had as yet formed any settled design in his own mind, but the tendency towards the course which eventually established the Protectorate is quite evident. To secure the rights of Englishmen and Christians rather than to strengthen the absolute supremacy of Parliaments had been his constant aim. Whether he reflected that if the monarchical power was to be given to some one not of the House of Stuart, it could hardly be given to any other man than himself, is a question which every one must answer as he thinks fit.

The conference had led to no decision, and during the first half of 1652 Cromwell had enough to do in defending religious liberty against those who had constituted themselves its champions. Before the Battle of Worcester had been fought, Parliament had passed a Blasphemy Act, for the punishment of atheistical, blasphemous and execrable opinions. In the following February, the publication of a Socinian catechism startled even the professed tolerationists. John Owen, the foremost Independent minister of the day, now—owing to the influence of Cromwell—Dean of Christchurch and Vice-Chancellor of the University of Oxford, was almost certainly the author of a scheme of ecclesiastical organisation presented by himself and twenty-six others to the Committee for the Propagation of the Gospel. This scheme in its main lines was subsequently adopted under the Protectorate. There was to be an established Church, ministered to by orthodox persons accepted by a body of triers, without regard to smaller points of discipline, on condition that they presented a testimonial "of their piety and soundness of faith," signed by six orthodox persons, and these ministers upon proof of unfitness were liable to be removed by a body of Ejectors. Other religious bodies were to be allowed to meet for worship, but Unitarians and those opposing the principles of Christianity were to be excluded from toleration. A list of fifteen fundamental propositions which no one was to be permitted to deny was set forth by Owen and his supporters. At this Cromwell took alarm. "I had rather," he said, "that Mahometism were permitted amongst us than that one of God's children be persecuted." The stand taken by him secured the warm approval of Milton. "Cromwell," wrote the poet, whose blindness had been hastened by his services to the State:

"Cromwell, our chief of men, who through a cloud
Not of war only, but detractions rude,
Guided by faith and matchless fortitude,
To peace and truth thy glorious way hast ploughed,
And on the neck of crownèd Fortune proud
Hast reared God's trophies, and his work pursued,
While Darwen stream with blood of Scots imbrued,
And Dunbar field resound thy praises loud,
And Worcester's laureate wreath: yet much remains
To conquer still; Peace hath her victories
No less renowned than War: new foes arise
Threatening to bind our souls with secular chains,
Help us to save free conscience from the paw
Of hireling wolves, whose Gospel is their maw."

Though Milton, in his unpractical idealism, was for discontinuing all public support to the clergy, whilst Cromwell, so far as we can judge, was merely for substituting some other mode of payment for the unequal burden of the tithe as it was levied in those days, they concurred on the point of extending religious liberty to the uttermost, and in this Cromwell had the army behind him. For the moment, however, the decision was postponed, as the Commonwealth had become involved in a war which occupied the thoughts of its rulers.

In the Dutch war, which broke out in 1652, neither Cromwell nor his brother officers had much part. Ever since the beginning of the Commonwealth a maritime war with France had virtually existed under the pretext of reprisals for injury done by French ships to English trade. The seizure of French goods in Dutch vessels had irritated the Netherlanders, and the Navigation Act passed in 1651 had taken away much of the trade done by them in English ports. In May, 1652, Tromp, the great Dutch admiral, had been sent out with orders to resist the right of search, and on approaching an English fleet commanded by Blake, he had neglected to lower his flag, as required by English commanders in satisfaction of their claim to enforce the Sovereignty over the British Seas, a claim which the Commonwealth had received from the Monarchy. An action resulting brought on war between the two peoples. In this war, neither Cromwell nor the army sympathised. Holding as they did that the force of England, if used at all, should be used for the advantage of Protestantism, they disliked a war waged against a Protestant nation. On the other hand they had no wish to see the English navy playing a craven part; and believing that Tromp had kept his flag flying as a studied insult, they offered no direct opposition to the war. Yet, as long as it was in progress, whenever any overture likely to lead to peace was made, it was sure to have the support of Cromwell and the officers.

If the Commonwealth leaders were immersed in preparations for war, the officers of the army had not forgotten their demand for reforms in Church and State, and in contemplating the slackness of Parliament with regard to these reforms, their minds were again set on a dissolution of Parliament at a time far earlier than that which had been fixed by the House itself. Towards the end of July the Army Council—now composed of officers alone—had considered a petition to be addressed to Parliament, and had asked "that a new representative be forthwith elected." When the petition was finally submitted to Parliament, this clause had given place to another merely requesting Parliament to consider of some qualifications which would secure "the election only of such as are pious and faithful in the interests of the Commonwealth to sit and serve as members in the said Parliament," in this way shifting from a demand for a dissolution to be followed by a general election, to a demand for partial elections to fill up existing vacancies. Though no direct evidence exists, there are strong reasons for believing that this substitution was made in consequence of Cromwell's intervention. Even then he did not append his signature to the petition.

It was as a mediator—not as a partisan—that Cromwell bore himself at the time when the army—after an interval of more than two years and a half—once more began to put pressure on Parliament. On the one hand Parliament was not only discredited by its inability to undertake the reforms demanded, but still more by the widely spread belief that many of its members had made full use of their opportunities to feather their own nests. On the other hand, this discredited House, though, mutilated as it was, it had scarcely a semblance of constitutional right, was yet the only body remaining in existence to which even a semblance appertained. Cromwell might not be an authority on constitutional law, but he had an instinctive apprehension for the truth on which all constitutional law is based—that the first thing necessary in the institutions of any country is not that they shall be theoretically defensible, but that they should meet with general acceptance. Those who like ourselves can look back on that stirring time from the safe vantage ground which we occupy, can see that, so far as constitutional questions were concerned, the work of the men of the seventeenth century was to substitute Parliament for the Crown as the basis of authority, and we have, accordingly, considerable difficulty in placing ourselves in the position of those to whom only part of the drama had been unrolled. In 1652, at least, it was impossible to appeal to the truncated Parliament as in any way representing the nation. Yet how was it possible to base authority on any new Parliament which should even approximate to such a representation? Except with extreme theorists there was no desire to evoke such a spectre. Already in 1650 Vane, speaking on behalf of the Parliamentary majority, had advocated a scheme of partial elections which left the members in possession of their seats, and the army leaders now proposed to substitute for this a general election modified by qualifications which would exclude all men of Royalist proclivities. The question at this time dividing Parliament and Army was therefore merely the choice of the best means of controlling the national verdict. The plan on either side might be one that men might reasonably adopt according to different points of view. Neither was likely to excite enthusiasm or to be generally accepted as a new basis of authority round which the nation could be expected to rally. There is no reason to suppose that Cromwell had anything better to propose, and it is certain that the theory, accepted at the present day, that it is better to allow a nation to learn by experience of misfortune than to force it, even to its own benefit, in a given direction, had no supporters in 1652, and least of all was it likely to find an advocate in Cromwell.

Cromwell had the strongest faith in the virtue of conferences at which such problems could be threshed out by men of good-will separated only by intellectual differences. It had been by an appeal to a committee that he had surmounted the difficulties which had faced him when the Levellers, in 1647, called prematurely for the trial of the King. He now, in October, 1652, secured the meeting of a conference between the leading members of Parliament and the principal officers. "I believe," he afterwards declared, "we had at least ten or twelve meetings, most humbly begging and beseeching of them that by their own means they would bring forth those good things which had been promised and expected; that so it might appear they did not do them by any suggestion from the army, but from their own ingenuity, so tender were we to preserve them in the reputation of the people." Vane and Bradshaw, and even, politically speaking, Henry Marten, the champions of the existing Parliament, were men of the highest character, and were justly apprehensive of giving way either to a military dictatorship, or to a Royalist reaction. Cromwell, on the other hand, had his eye increasingly fixed on the immediate evils of the present system. "How hard and difficult a matter was it," he complained at a somewhat later date, "to get anything carried without making parties, without things unworthy of a Parliament." In November he opened his mind to Whitelocke. "As for members of Parliament," he said, "the army begins to have a strange distaste against them, and I wish there were not too much cause for it; and really their pride and ambition, and their self-seeking, engrossing all places of honour and profit to themselves and their friends, and their daily breaking forth into new and violent parties and factions; their delay of business and design to perpetuate themselves and to continue the power in their own hands; their meddling in private matters between party and party contrary to the institution of Parliament, their injustice and partiality in those matters, and the scandalous lives of some of the chief of them; these things, my lord, do give much ground for people to open their mouths against them and to dislike them; nor can they be kept within the bounds of justice and law or reason, they themselves being the supreme power of the nation, liable to no account of any, nor to be controlled or regulated by any other power; there being none superior or co-ordinate with them." Cromwell was evidently harking back to his proposal for mixing something of monarchy with the existing institutions. "Unless," he continued, "there be some authority and power so full and so high as to restrain and keep things in better order, and that may be a check to these exorbitances, it will be impossible in human reason to prevent our ruin." To Whitelocke's constitutional objections he replied sharply: "What if a man should take upon him to be a King?" Whitelocke replied that it would be better to recall Charles II. Cromwell's utterance was plainly unpremeditated, and may be taken as a sign that the idea of his own elevation was, even at this early date, present in his mind, at least as a possibility, though it was far from having as yet crystallised itself into a settled design.

It was no restoration of kingship, but the speedy choice of

a new Parliament that was in the thoughts of Cromwell's subordinates. In January, 1653, a circular was sent by them to the regiments, asking the soldiers, as well as the officers, to approve of a petition for "successive Parliaments consisting of men faithful to the interests of the Commonwealth, men of truth, fearing God and hating covetousness," as well as for law reform and liberty of conscience. For some time it seemed as if Parliament would consent to hasten its own dissolution. In March, however, though a bill for new elections was considered, the pace slackened, and the hopes of the army again fell. In the army, indeed, there was far from being complete unanimity. A party headed by Lambert would have been content with a new Parliament from which members hostile to the Commonwealth were excluded, whilst the perfervid Harrison advocated the principles of the Fifth Monarchy, and asked that the government should be entrusted to moral and religious men, without recourse to popular election. Both Lambert and Harrison concurred in urging Cromwell to proceed to a forcible dissolution. Cromwell hesitated long. "I am pushed on," he complained, "by two parties to do that, the consideration of the issue whereof makes my hair stand on end."

If only Parliament could have been induced to clear the way for its successor on the terms proposed by the army, Cromwell would have been the first to rejoice. In the early part of April he was still prepared to stand by Parliament if it would proceed in earnest with the Bill for the new elections. Yet on the 6th, one of the days appointed for its consideration, the Bill was quietly passed over. By degrees it came out that the Bill, when completed, would be one authorising Vane's pet scheme of partial elections, the old members not only retaining their seats but forming an election committee with power to exclude any member whose presence was distasteful to them. There are even reasons to believe that it was intended that this arrangement should be a permanent one, and that each successive Parliament should have the right of shedding such members as were not to its taste. Moreover, as soon as the Bill was passed, Parliament was to adjourn till November, that it might be out of its power to repeal or amend the act under military pressure.

Such an arrangement must have irritated Cromwell to the uttermost. On April 15, having been absent from Parliament for a month, he returned to his place to plead against it. "It is high time," was the answer vouchsafed by one of the leading personages to his pleading for a new Parliament, "to choose a new general." Cromwell, in reply, offered his resignation, but as no officer could be found to take his place, the demand for it was soon dropped. Still anxious for a compromise, he made a fresh proposal. Why should not the difficulty be got over by a temporary suspension of the Parliamentary system, and a body of right-thinking men appointed to take into consideration the necessities of the time, and to prepare the way for its re-establishment. This proposal was taken into consideration at a meeting of officers and Parliamentarians on the 19th, but, as might have been expected, it provoked opposition and, after a sitting prolonged far into the night, the conference broke up on an undertaking given, as it would seem, by Vane, that the members of the House who were present would do their best to hinder the progress of the Bill on the following morning.

When the morning arrived, the House, taking the bit between its teeth, threw aside the engagements of its leaders and insisted on proceeding with the Bill. To the pecuniary interests of the Parliamentary rank and file it was far more important to escape the necessity of facing their constituents than it was to such men as Vane or Bradshaw, who would almost certainly be re-elected in any case. Yet it has never been alleged that either Vane or Bradshaw took steps to persuade the excited House to act in conformity with the promise given the evening before. Harrison at once despatched a message to Cromwell to warn him of the danger, and Cromwell evidently regarded the action of the members as a clear breach of faith on the part of Vane. Hurrying to the House, without giving himself time to change the plain black clothes and the grey worsted stockings which appear to have been considered unsuitable to a member in his place in Parliament, he sat for a while in silence. When the Speaker put the question that "this Bill do pass," he rose to speak.

Dwelling at first on the pains and care of the public good which had characterised the early days of the Long Parliament, he proceeded to blame the members for their later misconduct, holding up to scorn "their injustice, delays of justice, self-interest, and other faults . . . charging them not to have a heart to do anything for public good," and to have "espoused the corrupt interest of Presbytery and lawyers who were the supporters of tyranny and oppression." Their last crime was the present attempt to perpetuate themselves in power. "Perhaps," he continued, his wrath growing upon him as he spoke, "you think this is not Parliamentary language. I confess it is not, neither are you to expect any such from me." Then striding up and down the floor of the House, he pointed to individual members, charging them with corruption or immorality. "It is not fit," he added, "that you should sit as a Parliament any longer. You have sat long enough, unless you had done more good." Then, upon a remonstrance from Sir Peter Wentworth, he took the final step. "Come, come!" he cried, "I will put an end to your prating. You are no Parliament. I say you are no Parliament. I will put an end to your sitting." Then turning to Harrison, he uttered the fateful words, "Call them in; call them in." The door was thrown open and thirty or forty musketeers tramped in. "This," exclaimed Vane, "is not honest, yea it is against morality and common honesty." It was to Vane's broken word that Cromwell, whether truly or falsely, attributed the necessity of acting as he was now doing. Doubtless with a touch of sadness in his voice, he addressed his old friend—his brother, as he had long styled him—with the veiled reproof: "Oh, Sir Henry Vane! Sir Henry Vane! The Lord deliver me from Sir Henry Vane!"

The hall of meeting was soon cleared. Harrison handed Speaker Lenthall down from the chair. Algernon Sidney had to be removed with some show of compulsion. Most of the members, yielding to the inevitable, trooped out without even this nominal resistance. "It's you," said Cromwell as they filed past him, "that have forced me to this, for I have sought the Lord night and day that he would rather slay me than put me upon the doing of this work." Glancing at the mace he asked "What shall we do with this bauble?" Ordering Captain Scott to remove it from the table, he bade him take it away. When all was over, carrying the Bill on Elections under his cloak, he returned to Whitehall. In the afternoon he dispersed—in like manner—the Council of State, assuring its members that they could sit no longer, the Parliament having been dissolved. "Sir," replied Bradshaw, "we have heard what you did at the House in the morning, and before many hours all England will hear it; but Sir, you are mistaken to think that the Parliament is dissolved; for no power under heaven can dissolve them but themselves; therefore take you notice of that."

Chapter 5

The Nominated Parliament and the Protectorate

As at the trial of the King, so in the ejection of Parliament, Cromwell had been thrown back on the employment of military force. Legality was clearly against him on both occasions. Yet it must not be forgotten that he was the last to concur in the employment of force; and that there was much to be said for his assertion that the sitting members were no Parliament. Reduced by the flight of Royalists to the King in 1642 and by Pride's Purge in 1648, they had, after an existence of twelve years and a half, little remaining to them of that representative character which is the very being of a Parliament. At all events, this time, at least, Cromwell was secure of popular favour. Not a single voice was raised in defence of the expelled members. In the evening some wag scrawled on the door of the Parliament House: "This House to be let unfurnished." The Parliament disappeared amidst general derision. For all that, the work before Cromwell was one of enormous—perhaps even of hopeless—difficulty. Without Parliament or King, the nation was thrown upon its own resources to reconstruct its institutions as best it might. It was inevitable that in such stress of storm it should hark back to the old paths, and should see no prospect of settled government, save in the restoration of the throne, or at least in the election of another Parliament. Yet this was the very thing that Cromwell and all who were associated with him most dreaded. It was but too probable that such a solution would sweep away not only Puritanism, but all hope of political reform. Everything for which the army had fought and for which the nation had suffered was at stake, and it was not in human nature—certainly not in Cromwell's nature—to make such a sacrifice without a struggle. That such a struggle could only be prolonged with the support of the army was self-evident. Cromwell, however, was the last of men to desire to establish a purely military government, and the army, to do it justice, was commanded by men who were, for the most part, desirous to support their general in the experiment of establishing a civil government which would have dispensed with the interference of military power. The tragedy—the glorious tragedy—of Cromwell's subsequent career lay in the impossibility of permanently checking the instincts of military politicians to intervene in favour of those guarantees regarded by them as indispensable for the maintenance of the cause which they had so long upheld with all their might.

Distrust of the constituencies was the prominent feature of Cromwell's next move. The compromise offered by him of the temporary establishment of a non-elective body to prepare a basis of settlement whilst Parliamentary institutions remained in abeyance, was now adopted by the officers. Lambert,—who advocated a scheme for establishing a Council of State, apparently with provision for the increased independence of the executive, together with the election of a Parliament with restricted functions,—was unable to enforce his views. A small Council of State was established to carry on current affairs, but it was in the Council of Officers that the main question of the constitution was to be determined. Cromwell, after some hesitation, rallied to a very different scheme which had been suggested by Harrison, the brilliant soldier who dreaded to see the government in the hands of any but the Saints. Cromwell, however, whilst accepting Harrison's views on the whole, determined to modify them, in order to make the new assembly something more than a group of pious fanatics. He was consequently now anxious that it should include notable personages—even Fairfax was suggested—who had contended against the King, but who had no connection with the extreme sections of the community which found favour in Harrison's eyes. It was eventually resolved that the Council of Officers should invite nominations from the Congregational Churches in each county, reserving to itself the power of rejecting persons so named, and also of adding names which found no place on the list. On June 8 the persons finally selected received writs issued in the name of Cromwell as Lord General. An attempt had been made to secure the inclusion not only of Fairfax but of Vane, but neither of them would accept a place in the new assembly.

On July 4 the nominees of the army took their seats at Westminster. Cromwell, at all events, threw himself entirely into the spirit of the occasion. In a long speech he manifested his delight at seeing the government at last entrusted to the hands of the godly. No such authority, he proclaimed triumphantly, had ever before been entrusted to men on the ground that they owned God and were owned by Him. For once the emotional side of his nature had gained the upper hand over his practical common-sense. In long detail he told of the misconduct of the late Parliament, and repelled the idea that he had had any intention of substituting his own authority for that of the discarded House. It had been incumbent on him and his colleagues "not to grasp at the power ourselves, or to keep it in military hands, no, not for a day, but, as far as God enabled us with strength and ability, to put it into the hands of proper persons that might be called from the several parts of the nation." "This necessity," he proceeded to aver; "and I hope we may say for ourselves, this integrity of concluding to divest the sword of all power in civil administrations, hath been that that hath moved us to put you to this trouble." Then, enlarging on the providential character of the mission of the members of the new assembly, he urged them with many Scriptural quotations to take up their authority as men whom God had placed as rulers of the land. What, then, was to be said of that ideal of elected Parliaments, which had sunk so deeply into the minds of that generation? "If it were a time," he suggested, "to compare your standing with those that have been called by the suffrages of the people—which who can tell how soon God may fit the people for such a thing? None can desire it more than I! Would all were the Lord's people; as it was said, 'Would all the Lord's people were prophets': I would all were fit to be called." In time, indeed, this might be possible when the good and religious conduct of this assembly had won the people to the love of godliness. "Is not this the likeliest way to bring them to their liberties?" Finally, after much enforcement of the encouragements held forth by the Prophets and the Psalmists, he resigned all the power provisionally exercised by himself into the hands of his hearers, announcing to them that their power also was to be provisional. They were to hold it only till November 3, 1654, and then to give place to a second assembly to be elected by themselves—an assembly which was to sit for no more than a year, in which time it was to make provision for the future government of the country.

Contrary, as it would seem, to the intention of those by whom it had been called, the new assembly audaciously assumed the name of Parliament. Its real position being that of a mere body of nominees, Lilburne was once more brought into the field. In 1649 Lilburne had been tried and acquitted, but had subsequently been banished by the Long Parliament, which had added to its sentence a declaration that he would be guilty of felony if he, at any time, returned to England. He now reappeared in London, where he was sent to prison, again tried, and again acquitted. The line taken by him and his followers was that the so-called Parliament now in existence was no Parliament at all, as it was not elected by the people. With Cromwell's full consent, Lilburne was retained in confinement, being ultimately removed to Jersey, where no writ of habeas corpus could deliver him.

For a time Lilburne's attack consolidated the alliance between the Lord General and the nominees to whom political power had been entrusted. Yet it was not long before Cromwell's practical sense took alarm at their proceedings. It was indeed not the case, as has often been said, that the majority of the members were mere enthusiasts, but the enthusiasts settled down to Parliamentary work, seldom absenting themselves from the House, and being always ready to vote when a division was called; whilst those who distrusted them could not always be brought to a due sense of the importance of their Parliamentary duties, and were apt to be led away by interest or pleasure from supporting their opinions by their votes. Two questions were soon found to divide the parties, that of law reform, more especially the reform of Chancery, and that of a religious organisation other than compulsory uniformity under Bishops or Presbyters. On both these questions Cromwell was intensely interested, and there can be little doubt that if the nominated Parliament had conducted itself with due regard for practical exigencies, it would have retained his good-will to the end. Unfortunately this was not the case. It proposed a total abolition of the Court of Chancery, thus handing over to the hostile judges of the Common Law that system of equity which had been growing up with beneficial results for generations, whilst it also took in hand with a light heart the codification of the law, though not a single practising lawyer had a seat in the House, in the hope that "the great volumes of law would come to be reduced into the bigness of a pocket book." No wonder that Cromwell dropped into a friend's ear the words: "I am more troubled now with the fool than with the knave." No wonder either that in September he drew aside from Harrison, under whose influence he had decided in favour of summoning the nominees, and that he listened with greater respect to Lambert, the military representative of constitutionalism and the determined opponent of political fanaticism.

Cromwell's position was rendered difficult by his association with this ill-starred assembly. On September 14 a broadside was scattered in the streets charging him with treason to "his Lords the people of England," not because he had broken up the miserable remnant of the Long Parliament, but because he had stood in the way of the election of a new House, and it is highly probable that a large number of people who had nothing to do with the distribution of broadsides shared in this opinion. Still greater was the danger of an appeal to the army, with which the writers concluded. It was known that many of the soldiers, and even of the officers, were restive under the suspension of popular elections, and it was found necessary to secure submission by cashiering Lieutenant-Colonel Joyce, who had formerly, as a cornet, carried off the King from Holmby House, and who now threw himself on the side of those who cried out for constitutional rights.

On the subject of Church organisation, Parliament was as subversive as on the subject of law reform. Many of its members held with the Fifth Monarchy preachers, that the government of the State ought to be exclusively in the hands of the Saints, and, not unnaturally, concluded that they were themselves the Saints; thus taking a broad issue in defiance of the theory that the government ought to be administered or controlled by the elected representatives of the nation. The immediate dispute, however, turned on the unwillingness of the advanced party to continue any sort of endowment of the clergy. Cromwell, it is true, on more than one occasion had expressed himself strongly against the existing tithe system and would have been perfectly ready to concur in any plan for the removal of its abuses, or for substituting for it—as had been suggested in *The Agreement of the People* presented by the army—a more equitable mode of raising the money needed by the clergy. Further than that he was not likely to go, and matters were brought to a crisis by a resolution passed on November 17 for the abolition of patronage, and still more by the decision of the House on December 10—though only by a majority of two—to reject a scheme of Church government founded in the main on the lines drawn by Owen, in which the payment of tithes was taken as a financial basis.

Some time before the last vote was taken, the principal officers, under Lambert's leadership, had had under consideration a plan of a written constitution in which the executive power was to be strengthened and conferred upon Cromwell with the title of King, whilst the legislative power was to be conferred on an elected assembly, thus embodying the ideas which had been enunciated by Cromwell in his conference with the lawyers and politicians at the end of 1651. When this constitution was complete it was shown to Cromwell, who objected to the royal title, and who seems also to have been unwilling to have anything to do with another violent dissolution.

On December 10, when the vote on Church organisation was taken, Lambert and his allies found their opportunity. It is probable that they promised Cromwell that the House should be dissolved by its own action, and that, on receiving this assurance, he preferred not to be informed of the course by which this desirable end was to be attained. The course indeed was simple enough. The conservative reformers, if they chose to attend in anything like their full strength, were in a majority, and on the 12th they got up early and flocked to the House, where, before their bewildered opponents could rally in force, they immediately voted that Parliament should resign its powers into the hands of the Lord General. Then, starting for Whitehall in procession with the Speaker at their head, they announced to Cromwell the decision they had taken. Their advanced colleagues kept their seats, but upon attempting to remonstrate were expelled by a body of soldiers. As in the absence of the Speaker they could not technically be considered to be a House, those who interfered were able to aver, without literary untruthfulness, that there had been no forcible dissolution of Parliament.

In a very short time Cromwell had agreed with the officers on the constitution to be adopted under the name of *The Instrument of Government*. The executive power was to reside in a Lord Protector and Council, the members of which were to be appointed for life, Cromwell being named as the first Protector. The legislative power was assigned without restriction to a Parliament elected by constituencies formed, so far as the counties were concerned, upon a new franchise, the franchise in the boroughs being left in its old anomalous condition. This latter concession to prejudice was, however, of less importance, as a sweeping redistribution of seats, copied with little alteration from the scheme put forward in *The Agreement of the People,* largely increased the number of the county members, and disfranchised in equally large numbers the smaller boroughs which had fallen under the influence of the country gentlemen. The Parliament thus constituted was to meet once in three years and to sit at least for five months. Any Bill passed by this body was to be suspended for twenty days to give an opportunity for the Protector to explain objections he might entertain to it. If Parliament refused to listen to his objections, the Bill became law in spite of him, provided that it contained nothing contrary to the Instrument itself. The negative voice about which so much had been heard in the last years of Charles I was, therefore, not assigned to the Protector. For all that, the control over the executive is of greater importance to the development of representative institutions than legislative independence, and in this respect the hold of Parliament over the executive was of the flimsiest description, consisting merely of the right to propose six names whenever there was a vacancy in the Council, out of which the Council would select two, and the Protector again make his choice between the two. Even the financial arrangements, through which Parliaments usually make their way to power, were settled in such a way as to debar the elected House from obtaining even indirect control. It is true that the Instrument started with the sweeping generalisation that "no tax, charge, or imposition" was to be "laid upon the people but by common consent in Parliament," but this statement was followed by a clause assigning to the Protector £200,000 for civil expenses, besides as much as was needed for keeping up the navy, as well as an army of 30,000 men, and this sum, to which no definite limits were placed, was to be raised out of the customs "and such other ways and means as shall be agreed upon by the Protector and Council." As to the army and navy thus secured, the Protector was to dispose and order them with the consent of Parliament during its short session, but during all the rest of the three years with the consent of the Council only. It would, however, be a mistake to say that the Instrument established absolute government in England. The Protector was bound to act under the control of the Council, and though scarcely any record of the political action of that body has been preserved, there is enough to show that whilst Cromwell's personal influence over it was necessarily great, it was by no means a mere tool in his hands. The constitutional control to which the Protector was subjected was therefore a real one, though that control was in the hands of a body meeting in secret and sufficiently self-centred to make no bid for popularity by the speeches made in the course of discussions amongst its members, as a more popular assembly would have done. Finally, religious liberty was secured for all congregations which did not admit "Popery or Prelacy"; whilst the right of issuing ordinances with the force of law was granted to the Protector and Council till the first Parliament met.

It has frequently been urged that the Instrument was the earliest example of that system of fixed constitutions, of which the most notable instance is that of the United States, and must therefore rank with such constitutions rather than with the system of Parliamentary supremacy which was ultimately adopted in England. The comparison with the American constitution, however, can only stand with those who are resolved to fix their attention on similarities and to ignore differences. The Instrument, it is true, resembles the Constitution of the United States in refusing to submit the holders of executive authority to the constant control of the legislature, and in setting forth the relations between the bodies of the State in a written document. On more important points there is a world-wide distinction. In America, the whole federal constitution is redolent of popular control. Every four years the President is re-elected or replaced, and though Congress cannot dismiss a President except by a judicial impeachment, it has complete control over the finances, and can leave him without supply. Add to this the ingrained habit of the American people in giving vent to popular opinion, and in pressing it on the notice of the government which it has given to itself, and we shall find little cause to seek in the Constitution of the United States for a justification of the Instrument—a document drawn up by soldiers and endowing the chief of the State and his councillors with a lifelong tenure of office, with an abundant armed force, and with a power of taxation adequate to all ordinary requirements in time of peace. The question raised by the Instrument was not whether the national control was to be exercised indirectly through Parliament, or directly through a popular vote, but whether it should be exercised at all. The constitutional principles alike respected in England and America are diametrically opposed to those on which the government of the Protectorate was founded.

On December 16, 1653, Oliver was installed at Westminster as Lord Protector under the conditions of the Instrument. His Council consisted of seven officers and eight civilians, the most notable of the latter being Sir Anthony Ashley Cooper —better known by the title long afterwards conferred on him by Charles II as the Earl of Shaftesbury—who had been an active member of the Councils formed after the break-up of the Long Parliament. Little as is known of his actions during this period of his life, his rallying to the Protectorate can only be explained as the result of the conviction that Oliver was in earnest in his intention of giving to the new government a preponderatingly civilian character, and of keeping it out of the hands of fanatics on one hand, and of soldiers on the other. In Thurloe, who had acted as Secretary to the Council since the spring of 1652, the Protector acquired an official whose ability was beyond dispute, who was appalled by no labours, and one who, with the aid of the network of spies whose poverty he utilised, was keen-sighted in penetrating the secrets of conspirators at home and abroad.

The Protectorate was at least placed beyond immediate danger by the adhesion of the army and the fleet. Scarcely less important was the concurrence of the judges, amongst them that honourable man and eminent lawyer Matthew Hale, who had won Oliver's approbation by his services in the cause of law-reform. Hale, indeed, informed the Protector that as he was personally desirous of seeing a Royalist restoration, he could only remain on the bench on the condition that he should be excused from taking part in the trials of political prisoners. Oliver at once gave the required promise. The compromise was creditable to both the parties concerned.

The Protector, by his assumption of the government, had roused up enemies enough to make him chary of dispensing with the support of so valuable a helper. To the Royalists, who hoped to strike at a single person more easily than at a Parliament, were added the Fifth Monarchy preachers, who held that Oliver was "the vile person to whom they shall not give the honour of the kingdom," but who should "come in peaceably and obtain the kingdom by flatteries," as foretold by the Prophet Daniel. They were the more dangerous as they were known to have supporters in the army, especially as Harrison, who shared their opinions, had been thought of by the advanced members of the nominated Parliament as a possible substitute for Oliver in the command. The first repressive action of the Protectorate was therefore to place two of the most turbulent of the preachers under lock and key, and to deprive Harrison of his commission. Such men were only really dangerous by their hold on a portion of the army, whilst the Commonwealth's men, such as Bradshaw and Vane, though not in the least likely to head an armed resistance, were strong in the conviction which they shared with a considerable number of their countrymen, that the only possibility of defence against the evils of military rule was to be found in a recurrence to legality. It is true that with them legality consisted in the restoration of a sovereign Parliament, whilst the Royalists saw it in the restoration of the King, but if ever time and circumstances should fuse the two ideas together, a body of opinion would be created which would try to the uttermost the fabric of a government raised on other principles.

Oliver's task was necessarily conditioned by the nature of the opposition he had to encounter. His new system, if it were to have a chance of becoming permanent, would have to commend itself to that large majority of men who follow no ideals, but are content to live under any rule, whatever may have been its origin, if only the rulers confer upon them a reasonable amount of protection, and are sufficiently in sympathy with the governed to be regarded with love rather than with fear. It was this quality that had mainly helped Elizabeth to make a doubtful legal position a step in her triumphant career, and it was to Elizabeth alone amongst recent English sovereigns that Oliver looked with respect and admiration. Nor was he deficient in many of the characteristics which had made Elizabeth great. He had the same patriotism, the same skill in the selection of agents, the same impatience of partisan bitterness in Church and State, the same readiness to trust in the healing virtues of time. The chief obstacles in the way of a repetition of Elizabeth's success lay, not merely in the stain of the king's blood upon his hands, but also in his leadership of an army of which the officers shaped their conduct in accordance with distinct religious and political ideas. He had risen to power by the sympathy of these men. Was it possible to secure the sympathy of the nation without alienating the army to the support of which he must look till he could place his authority on a wider basis?

In the first and easiest portion of the task before the Protector, the redress of grievances weighing upon the people, there was no hesitation. The Instrument had conferred upon Oliver and his Council the right of issuing ordinances with the force of law up to the meeting of Parliament; and in little more than eight months no fewer than eighty-two of these ordinances had been issued subject to amendment, if Parliament chose to interfere. The Council was, in fact, like the Cabinet of to-day, far more capable of initiating legislation than a Parliament consisting of several hundred members, and that so little criticism attended these ordinances may be taken as satisfactory evidence that there was good reason for that strengthening of the government which had been the main argument of the founders of the new constitution. The ordinance for the reform of Chancery was certainly exposed to the conservative objections of the lawyers and was, no doubt, susceptible of improvement, but it aimed at the removal of acknowledged abuses, especially at accelerating the movements of a Court whose long delays had caused that wide-spread irritation which had given support even to the exaggerated proposals of the nominated Parliament.

Still more important was the adoption of the new scheme of Church government. The minister presented to a living was required to have a certificate of fitness from three persons of known godliness and integrity, one of them being a settled minister; afterwards he was to hand this certificate to certain commissioners known as Triers and to obtain their testimony that he was "a person for the grace of God in him, his holy and unblamable conversation, as also for his knowledge and utterance, able and fit to preach the gospel." Having become an incumbent, he was liable to expulsion by a local body of Ejectors for immorality or for holding blasphemous or atheistical opinions. As long as he was maintained in his post, he might uphold any Puritan system he pleased and organise his congregation on the Presbyterian, Independent, or Baptist system, if he could persuade them to follow him. Those persons, whether lay or clerical, who objected to the system upheld in their parish church, were at liberty to form separate congregations—gathered Churches, as they were called—at their own discretion. Later on, towards the close of 1655, Oliver's tolerant spirit gave way to the return of the Jews, who had been exiled from England since the reign of Edward I. A few Unitarians were no doubt excluded from the benefits of his toleration. Moreover, the Society of Friends, now rising into importance under the leadership of George Fox, was also threatened with exclusion as presumably guilty of blasphemy, though the Protector himself not infrequently interfered on behalf of its members. Even if this had been otherwise, the Society put in no claim for participation in a legal support or even for acknowledgement by the State.

That the Church thus constituted was but a Puritan Church is the charge commonly brought against the system of the Protectorate. That it was so is certainly not to be denied, but, after all, it must be remembered that, so far as opposition to Puritanism was based on definite religious grounds, and not merely on moral slackness, it was confined to a comparatively small number of Englishmen. Before the days of Laud, the clergy of the Church had been for the most part, so far as their teaching was concerned, Puritan in their ideas, and lax in their ceremonial observances, and thus the ecclesiastical changes initiated by the Long Parliament had been received by the bulk of the laity rather as the removal of innovations than as the establishment of something entirely new. The honour in which episcopacy and the Prayer Book were now held was mainly confined to the Royalist gentry and to scholars expelled from the Universities, and was therefore understood to be closely connected with political aims. Even so, there was no attempt as yet on the part of the Government to suppress the use of the Prayer Book in private houses, and there is reason to suppose that if no political disturbances had followed, no such attempt would have been made at a later time. The system of the Protectorate was undoubtedly the most tolerant yet known in England—more tolerant, indeed, than public opinion would, if left to itself, have sanctioned.

Not only by its legal reforms did the Protectorate strive to commend itself to the nation. Oliver had never thrown his heart into the Dutch war, and a little before he dissolved the Long Parliament, a great English victory in a battle which began off Portland and ended under Cape Grisnez, had secured the mastery over the Channel to the English fleet. That fleet rallied to the new Government; even Blake, who was hostile at first, accepting the result of political changes, and finally throwing in his lot with the Protectorate, on the ground that it was the business of the navy to leave politics alone, and —though the expression is not traceable on sufficient evidence to Blake's lips—"to keep foreigners from fooling us." The wound that Blake received off Portland incapacitated him from taking a considerable part in the later battles of the war, the burden lying for the most part on Monk, who won victories off the Gabbard in June and off the Texel in July, not long after the nominated Parliament had entered on its unlucky career. In the latter conflict, Tromp, the great Dutch admiral whose ill success was due not to any failure of his powers or to any want of manliness in his crews, but to the inefficiency of the Government he served, was killed by a shot as he was entering into the battle. Even whilst the nominated Parliament was still in session, a negotiation with the Dutch had been opened, and this negotiation, which was countenanced by Oliver from the first and carried on earnestly by him as Protector, ended in a peace signed on April 5, 1654.

Those who wish to estimate the value of Oliver's foreign policy and its bearing upon the fortunes of the government he hoped to establish will do well to study at length the story of his negotiation with the Dutch, and of his contemporary excursions into the domain of Continental affairs. It is beyond doubt that he was desirous of peace with the Dutch on the ground that they were Protestants, and that he was also desirous of allying himself with other Protestant States for the protection of Protestants under persecution by Roman Catholic Governments. Yet, not only did this fail to hinder him from exacting hard terms from the Dutch, but the motive of his diplomacy is revealed in his eagerness to make an agreement with his actual enemies a step to immediate hostilities with other nations. At one time he proposed a plan for the partition between England and the Netherlands of so much of the globe as lies outside Europe whilst he was at the same time negotiating with the Governments of France and Spain, offering to make common cause with one or the other in the war then raging between them. No doubt some religious element could be imported into either quarrel. To help Spain against France, at least in the way he proposed, was to vindicate the French Protestants against a persecution to which they were to some extent exposed, in spite of the acceptance by their Government of the Edict of Nantes. To assist France against Spain was to weaken the most bigoted Roman Catholic Government in existence.

What we are here concerned with, however, is not the details of Oliver's foreign policy, but its conception as a whole. It is true that the existing position of affairs in Europe,—in which France and Spain were neutralising the forces of one another—was almost an invitation to the strong military and naval power of the Protectorate to extend its influence at the expense of one or other of the rivals; but, so far as this consideration may have played its part in bringing Oliver to a decision, it has left no traces in his recorded words. Obviously, when he undertook the negotiation with the Dutch, he had two courses before him, either to lay the foundations of a general peace, or to leave himself free to push military and naval enterprises in other directions. It was the latter course on which he resolved—a course which has gained him the admiration of a posterity prompt to recognise in Oliver the ruler who, having received from the Commonwealth an excellently organised army and navy, was the first to apply those potent instruments of conquest to the acquisition of over-sea dominion. What posterity has failed to observe is that this design was incompatible with his other design of settling the government of England on a constitutional basis. By his resolve to seek military employment for the magnificent force that he had welded together, and to find reasons for going to war with some nation or other, rather than be driven into war by the necessity of upholding the honour and interests of the country, Oliver was compelled to keep up a military and naval establishment which may not have been in excess of the taxable capacity of the nation; but which at all events imposed a burden much heavier than that to which Englishmen had been accustomed to submit. Before Parliament met, after many hesitations he had resolved to send out one fleet under Blake into the Mediterranean to enforce the release of English prisoners taken by the pirates of the Barbary coast, and another fleet under Penn to seize upon Hispaniola or some other West Indian island as a response to the refusal of Spain to allow English merchantmen to trade even with English colonies in the West Indies, as well as to various acts of violence already committed by Spanish officials in American waters.

That in both these cases Oliver was justified in seeking redress can hardly be denied. As regards Spain, he had already made a twofold demand on Cardenas, the Spanish ambassador, first, for liberty of trade in the Indies—not necessarily, so far as our information goes, for liberty of trade with Spanish possessions—and, secondly, for entire liberty of religion for English merchants and sailors in their own houses on Spanish soil and in their ships in Spanish ports—he not being satisfied with the offer of Spain to renew the stipulations of the treaty signed by Charles I, in which the Inquisition was debarred from acting against English Protestants so long as they created no scandal. Both demands were promptly rejected. "It is," replied Cardenas, "to ask my master's two eyes." Oliver's notion that he could attack a Spanish colony in the West Indies and yet remain at peace with Spain can only be explained by his admiration for Elizabethan methods, which led him to suppose that the existing Spanish Government would be as ready as that of Philip II to put up with a system which kept peace in Europe whilst war was being waged in America. It is not, however, with problems of international morality that we are at present concerned. Before Blake could sail for the Mediterranean or Penn for the West Indies, Parliament would meet, and would be confronted with the fact that, in addition to his fleets, the Protector had on foot a land force of 57,000 men, a number exceeding by no less than 27,000 the 30,000 which the Instrument itself had laid down as the normal strength of the army. It is true that he could hardly have met his engagements with a smaller force. Ireland was only recently subdued; and insurrection against the English conquerors—known as Glencairn's rising—was in full swing in Scotland; the dread of a Royalist movement in England required the maintenance of more troops than would be needed in quieter times, whilst other regiments were already preparing for embarkation in the West Indian fleet. On the other hand, when it is remembered that it was through his command of the services of these soldiers that Oliver had been raised to power, that he could still count on their support to maintain him in it, and that he was calling upon the nation to bear the burden of enterprises which he had originated without asking its consent, can it be matter of wonder that at such a time there should be some effort on the part of a Parliament which had come to look upon itself as representing the nation to impose limits upon the burdens which had already far outgrown even the prescriptions of the Instrument itself?

The elections to the first Protectorate Parliament were held under peculiar conditions. In the boroughs still permitted to return members the old conditions existed, but in the counties to which a redistribution of seats had transferred the electoral power, hitherto possessed by small villages under the influence of the neighbouring landowners, the Instrument had established a uniform franchise of the ownership of real or personal property worth £200. So far as we can trace any direct issue before the constituencies, the elections turned on the approval or renunciation of the policy of the advanced party in the nominated Parliament, and on this the electorate gave no uncertain sound. That party was practically swept away, and a full approbation thereby accorded to the conservative policy which had been the main strength of the appeal made to the country by the new government. It did not follow that the new constitution would meet with the same approbation. A not inconsiderable number of the Commonwealth men, such as Bradshaw and Hazlerigg, sore at their expulsion from the benches of the Long Parliament, had been returned, together with a goodly company of political Presbyterians, who might be expected to do their best to free Parliament from the shackles of the Instrument.

Under these circumstances, Oliver's speech at the opening of Parliament was a masterpiece of skill. Dwelling on the points on which he and the majority of his hearers were in agreement, he kept out of sight those on which differences might arise. He called for healing and settlement, for orderly government which might replace the confusions of the past and stem the tide of fanaticism in the present. He dwelt not on the extent of the liberty of conscience proclaimed in the Instrument, but on the restrictions imposed in that document, especially on such teachers as "under the profession of Christ, hold forth and practise licentiousness." He held up for acceptance the doctrine that, when such a result was to be feared, it was the duty of the magistrate to intervene. He protested against the notion that it was antichristian for a minister to receive ordination, and also against the notion that the Fifth Monarchy was about to commence, and that it was "for men, on this principle, to betitle themselves that they are the only men to rule kingdoms, govern nations, and give laws to people, and determine of property and liberty and everything else." Then came Oliver's appeal for support on the grounds of the difficulties he had inherited from his predecessors—troubles in Ireland and Scotland, trade with Portugal and France interrupted, as well as a war with the Dutch; after which he set forth the benefits of the Instrument, the legal and ecclesiastical reforms it had rendered possible, the peace with the Dutch, and the commercial treaties concluded with Sweden and Denmark. Finally came a hint that Parliament might well be liberal with its supplies, as in spite of the enormous burdens weighing upon it, the Government had diminished, by no less than £30,000 a month, the assessment tax by which army and navy were in part supported. It has often been doubted whether Oliver had in him the making of a Parliamentary tactician. Those who reply in the affirmative may point to this speech in defence of their opinion, especially if we accept the evidence of the Dutch ambassadors that Oliver—in words subsequenty omitted from the published speech—concluded by a direct invitation to the House to take into consideration the Instrument, no doubt expecting its easy acceptance by men who were as desirous of order as himself. Confirmatory of this conclusion is the fact that when the Parliamentary debates opened and the question was asked whether the House was prepared to leave the government under the control of a single man, it was a member of the Council who demanded that all other business should be laid aside till the Instrument had been submitted to the approval of the House.

When this demand had been complied with, it became evident that the majority of the members were in favour of imposing further restrictions on the Protector which would make him no more than a tool in the hands of Parliament. Such a position Oliver absolutely declined to accept, and on its being known that Harrison had been seeking the advantage of his own party by stirring up confusion at Westminster, and had boasted that he would have 20,000 men at his back, he struck firmly and sharply. Harrison was sent for under guard, and Parliament was ordered to attend the Protector in the Painted Chamber.

The speech which the Protector delivered to the members may rank as the ablest which is known to have fallen from his lips. There can be no doubt that he would personally have preferred the retention of the Instrument as it stood, but he was aware of the objections taken to it, and all that we know leads us to believe that those objections were shared by members of his own Council. At all events, after a justification of his own conduct in relation to the preparation of the Instrument, and an argument that it had been accepted by the electors who had been bound by its terms to acknowledge the settlement of the government in a single person and Parliament, he proceeded to offer a compromise. He was prepared to substitute for the Instrument a Parliamentary constitution, provided that four conditions were admitted as fundamentals to be handed down to posterity as unassailable. The first was that the country was to be governed by a single person and a Parliament; the second, that Parliaments were not to make themselves perpetual; the third, that liberty of conscience should be respected; the fourth, that neither Protector nor Parliament should have absolute power over the militia. It speaks volumes for Oliver's power of seeing into the heart of a situation, that whilst the Instrument of Government, and the absolute supremacy of a single House with power to defy dissolution, have alike passed into the realms of unrealised theory, every one of Oliver's fundamentals has been adopted by the nation—not indeed in any written constitution, but with the stronger and more enduring guarantee of a practice accepted beyond dispute by the conscience of the people itself. The four fundamentals on behalf of which he now appealed to the House formed the political legacy bequeathed by him to posterity.

To obtain acquiescence in this compromise, Oliver directed that no member should take his seat who refused to sign the following declaration: "I do hereby freely promise and engage to be true and faithful to the Lord Protector and the Commonwealth of England, Scotland and Ireland, and shall not, according to the tenor of the indentures whereby I am returned to serve in this present Parliament, propose or give my consent to alter the Government as it is settled in one person and a Parliament." Those who refused subscription were excluded from all participation in the business of the House.

The imposition of such a restriction was doubtless condemnable on the principle that the will of the electorate expressed through its representatives must be taken as final in all disputes. Neither Cromwell, however, nor his opponents had recognised such a principle. Vane and Bradshaw had been ready to exclude Royalists, and other unfit persons, whilst the authors of the Instrument had imposed qualifications with a very similar object. If a test there was to be, the one now selected was not only the lightest possible, but it was one that had already been signed by each constituency on behalf of its members, without which formality they were not, according to the Instrument, entitled to take their seats. It left them perfectly at liberty to propose any amendment of the constitution, even to vote against any one of Oliver's fundamentals with the exception of the first.

It is impossible here to enter into details of the constitutional debates which followed. It is sufficient to say that the basis which Parliament proposed to substitute for the Instrument was the revival of the negative voice, so that no constitutional innovation could be made without the Protector's consent. Of the four fundamentals, the first two—the one relating to the position of the single person and the other refusing to Parliament the right of perpetuating itself—were accepted without opposition. The other two raised greater difficulties. The House was very far from being anxious to extend religious liberty as widely as the Protector desired, but it ultimately agreed to a form of words which practically left the decision in his hands. The absolutely insurmountable difficulty was found in the disposal of the army. In the first place, Parliament held out for the diminution of the numbers of the regular forces to the 30,000 men allowed by the Instrument, and required that if more were needed they should be raised in the form of a militia which would fall more readily under the influence of the local gentry. In the second place, the House resolved to limit its grant of supply to the taxation required for the maintenance of the army for a term of five years only, thus reserving to itself the ultimate financial control which spells sovereignty. Cromwell's whole soul recoiled from the acceptance of a scheme which would render nugatory the proposed constitutional restrictions of Parliamentary omnipotence, by enabling Parliament, at the end of the assigned term, to stop the supplies without which the army could not be maintained; unless indeed, when that term reached its end, the Protector chose to employ his army to crush the Parliament of 1659 as he had employed it to crush the Parliament of 1653. Parliamentary supremacy or military despotism were the alternatives which Oliver or his successor would have to face in the not very distant future.

If two men ride on one horse, one of them must ride in front, and this sober physical truth is equally applicable to the realm of politics. No paper constitution, however deserving of veneration, can prevent there being some force in every nation capable of making itself supreme if it chooses to do so. It may be the constituencies, as in England at the end of the nineteenth century; the people consulted in mass, as in the United States; or the army, as in England in the middle of the seventeenth century. Such supremacy may be subjected to the checks of written or unwritten constitutions, and may be thus thrust into the background till called forth by some special crisis; but in the long run it is impossible to prevent supreme power from exerting itself. The defect of Oliver's fourth fundamental was that it sought to divide the control of the army, or, in other words, Sovereignty, between Protector and Parliament, at a time when the Protector was powerless to act in defiance of the army. It is useless to deny that he was perfectly in the right in hesitating to hand over supreme power to a Parliament uncontrolled by the nation, and capable of using its financial authority to demolish any system of government that might stand in the way of the ambitions of its members. It is equally undeniable that, as he was unable to depend on the nation as a whole, he had nothing to fall back upon except a Protectorate which, in reality, was controlled by the will of the leading officers, who found in the provisions of the Instrument which they had themselves originated the means of perpetuating their own power by securing—irrespective of the concurrence of Parliament or nation—the levy of taxes, the amount of which was fixed by the Protector and Council alone.

Oliver having once made up his mind to refuse his consent to the new constitution, was anxious to hasten the dissolution of the Parliament. The Instrument having provided that the House should sit for five months, he opportunely remembered that the months by which the army's pay was regulated were lunar months; and on January 22, 1655, when five lunar months were expired, he pronounced its dissolution. The speech in which he announced his determination was stamped with vexation of spirit at the failure of his hopes, a vexation in itself by no means unjustifiable. The tragedy of the situation lay in the undoubted fact that however much they might differ on the means to be pursued, the end at which Protector and Parliament aimed was identical, namely, the conversion of the military into the civil state. Parliament had counted it well done to leave Oliver in possession for five years, whilst Oliver, conscious of his own rectitude of purpose, and ignoring the consideration that at the end of five years he might no longer be living, and that the Protectorate might have passed by demise into less worthy hands, complained that he was not trusted. Why, he asked, had they not come to him to talk the matter over? Why indeed, except that Parliaments have their pride as well as Protectors, and that this one had come to the conclusion that it was its duty to settle the constitution rather than to accept a settlement from a knot of soldiers. If it did no seek an opporunity to discuss such grave questions with Oliver in person, at least it had had the advantage of listening to what might be presumed to be his views when promulgated by those members of his Council who were also members of the House.

In an elaborate defence of the Instrument, Oliver put his finger on the real ground of offence. "Although," he declared in speaking of the rights of the Protector, "for the present the keeping up and having in his power the militia seems the most hard, yet, if it should be yielded up at such a time as this when there is as much need to keep this cause by it—which is evidently at this time impugned by all the enemies of it—as there was to get it, what would become of all? Or if it should not be equally placed in him and the Parliament, but yielded up at any time, it determines the Power," *i.e.*, hinders the exercise of authority by the person in possession of power, "either from doing the good he ought, or hindering Parliaments from perpetuating themselves, or from imposing what religion they please on the consciences of men, or what government they please upon the nation; thereby subjecting us to dis-settlement in every Parliament, and to the desperate consequences thereof: and if the nation shall happen to fall into a blessed peace, how easily and certainly will their charge be taken off, and their forces disbanded; and then, where will the danger be to have the militia thus stated?"

It was impossible for the Protector to put his case more convincingly. Yet, admirable as a criticism pointing out the danger likely to follow on the adoption of the proposals of Parliament, Oliver's reasoning pre-supposed the acceptance by Parliament of his own conviction that an armed minority had the right to impose its principles on the unarmed majority—the very belief which the authors of the Parliamentary constitution were most determined to resist. Even if it had been possible for any Puritan party to look for a solution of the problem in an appeal to the unfettered judgment of the nation, it is evident that Oliver would never have agreed to such an arbitration. On the one side was the resolve to get what appeared to be the right thing done, if necessary by force. On the other side was the resolve to eliminate the element of force by subordinating it to the rule of Parliaments. For the moment the decisive word rested with Oliver. "I think myself bound," he said in conclusion, "as in my duty to God, and to the people of these nations, for their safety and good in every respect—I think it my duty to tell you that it is not for the profit of these nations, nor for common and public good for you to continue longer, and therefore I do declare unto you, that I do dissolve this Parliament."

History has pronounced in favour of the view taken by Oliver's antagonists. The reliance on military power in which he had found his refuge did more than all other facts put together to establish, for good or for evil, a reliance on Parliament. It is the special mark of his greatness that he put his whole heart after the dissolution of his first Parliament into an effort to avoid the appearance even of a temporary dictatorship. He shrank from being a military ruler, even under the plea of the necessity of the times. His holding back the dissolution of Parliament till the fifth month—lunar month as it was—had been accomplished, offers the key-note of the position as he judged it. The Parliamentary constitution had perished stillborn. The constitution of the Instrument was in full force, and was to be observed, even though it were to his own detriment. The Instrument enabled the Protector and Council to levy such taxation as they thought fit for 30,000 men and for a navy sufficient for defence, whilst he had now on foot some 57,000 soldiers, and, in addition to the home fleet, two others had already been despatched—the one to the Mediterranean, the other to the West Indies. Yet the Protector was able to announce that he would content himself with levying the Assessment money at the low amount of £80,000 a month on the three nations, an amount which the dissolved Parliament had fixed as sufficient for the forces named in the Instrument. Such a decision left the Government with enormous forces—as forces were in those days reckoned—which it had no visible means of paying; but it was an announcement in the most practical form, that, as soon as the existing situation would admit, the military expenditure should be brought down to the requirements of the Instrument. The announcement was accompanied by a proclamation setting forth the principles on which the Protector had decided to act on the thorny question of religious liberty. There was to be complete freedom for all who contented themselves with setting forth their opinions, without "imposing" on the conscience of others or disturbing their worship. The last clause, which was aimed at the new Society of Friends, commonly styled Quakers by the irreverent multitude, sought to put a stop to their practice of carrying on their polemics in churches where congregations were assembled. To the exhortations of George Fox himself the Protector listened with respect. "Come again to my house," said Oliver, "for if thou and I were but an hour a day together, we should be nearer one to the other. I wish you no more ill than I do to my own soul." A reverence for genuineness, in whatever shape, was not the least admirable of Oliver's characteristics.

The clause against "imposing" was more widely sweeping in its aims. It struck at the claims of the Roman Papacy, and the English episcopacy, as well as at the designs of the late Parliament to establish lists of opinions to which toleration should be refused. It struck also at all attempts to snatch at political power with the object of serving religious ends. Oliver's breach with Parliament had roused attacks from every quarter. There were the Fifth Monarchy men who rejected every form of secular government and whose leaders were not to be silenced except by placing them under guard. Harrison himself had to be placed under arrest. It was not work that Oliver would have chosen. "I know," wrote Thurloe, "it is a trouble to my Lord Protector to have any one that is a saint in truth to be grieved or dissatisfied with him." The Cavaliers might be regarded as hereditary enemies. In the last summer a Cavalier plot to assassinate the Protector had been discovered, and two of the plotters, Gerard and Vowel, had been executed. Whilst Parliament was still in session, Thurloe's spies—who were to be found in every land in which their services were required—brought him news of a projected insurrection, and it had been one of Oliver's charges against the members, that their delay in settling the government had fostered the plot. In March futile attempts to rise were made in various parts of the country, the only one which gained the dignity of an actual insurrection being that in which Penruddock and other gathered in arms at Salisbury, seized the judges of assize in their beds and marched off in the hope of rallying the scattered Royalists of the west. The insurgents, however, were dispersed in Devonshire, where many of them were captured. In the end a few of the ringleaders were tried and executed, whilst a large number of their adherents were transported without legal trial to Barbados. Such procedure, whether it be counted as an evasion or as a breach of the law, was evidence of the difficulty which Oliver would increasingly feel in meeting his enemies otherwise than by the exertion of arbitrary power.

A more difficult question arose when two judges sent to try Royalist prisoners in the north doubted their competency, on the ground that an ordinance defining the offences constituting treason, which the Protector, in accordance with the Instrument, had issued before the meeting of Parliament, could not make a rebellion against the Protectorate to be High Treason. The two judges were at once dismissed, and soon afterwards Chief Justice Rolle was compelled to resign office because he was unwilling to enforce the payment of customs upon a certain Cony; whilst the three lawyers who argued on Cony's behalf—one of them being Serjeant Maynard, who lived to welcome William III—that he was not to pay duties imposed by Protector and Council without the consent of Parliament, were sent to prison till they had apologised. One historian after another has accompanied his account of these proceedings with the observation that there was here a conflict between law and the tyrant's plea, necessity. There was nothing of the sort. The question was whether the Instrument was a valid constitution. If it was, there could be no reasonable doubt that rebels against the Protectorate were legally traitors, or that customs-duties applicable to the payment of the army and navy were legally set, not by Parliament, but by Protector and Council.

If all that Oliver and his councillors had asked of the Instrument had been to enable them to carry on the government till the lapse of three years drove them to summon another Parliament, they might have been well content. They could not, however, forget that they were the leaders of the party of reform, and the Instrument itself had deprived them of the power of initiating reforms except through Parliament. The authority to issue ordinances with the force of law had ceased with the meeting of Parliament, and all that could now be done was to urge the Commissioners of the Great Seal to carry out the ordinance for the reform of Chancery, and, upon their refusal, to replace them by others likely to be more complacent. The result was a movement in opposition to the Instrument amongst some of Oliver's partisans, by which he was hampered as well as assisted. It was natural that such a movement should also have the character of opposition to the military party from whom the Instrument had proceeded. Already in the late Parliament an unsuccessful effort had been made to confer the title of King on Oliver in the hope that the civilian element in the Government would be thereby strengthened. In the summer of 1655 a petition was circulated in the City asking the Protector to assume legislative power on the invitation of the subscribers. Oliver was far too prudent to follow such a will-of-the-wisp, and the petition was suppressed by the Council. The needs that had called it forth could not so easily be dismissed, especially as the Protector's desire to reform abuses was strongly reinforced by his need of money—a need which was dramatically exhibited when the soldiers of his guard broke into his kitchen and carried off the dinner cooked for his own table, telling him to his face that as they had not received their pay, they had taken some of it in kind.

If Oliver was to make both ends meet, it could only be by reductions in the army, and to effect these he needed the co-operation of the officers, whilst so far as Scotland and Ireland were concerned, reductions which might have been dangerous in January had ceased to be dangerous in July. Monk, who had been sent back to the north as soon as he could be spared from the Dutch war, had reduced the Highlands to submission; and Ireland, which had been earlier subjected by English arms, was now to have imposed on her that thorough-going system of English colonisation which is usually known as the Cromwellian settlement, the principles of which had, however, been laid down by preceding Governments. Those of the landowning class who were unable to prove, to the satisfaction of English judges, that they had shown constant good affection to the English Government, even if they had taken no part against England in the late war—that is to say, the great bulk of the class which had anything to lose amongst the Irish Catholics—were driven off into the devastated lands of Connaught, and their estates were divided amongst English soldiers and other Englishmen who had lent money for the support of the war upon the security of confiscated land. Henceforth there was to be in three of the Irish provinces a class of landed proprietors of English birth and the Protestant religion, surrounded by peasants and labourers who were divided from them by racial and religious differences of the most extreme kind. Such an arrangement boded ill for the future peace of the country. The immediate result was untold misery to the sufferers and the kindling of hope in English bosoms that at last Ireland would be peopled by a race loyal to the institutions and religion of her conquerors.

In any case the scheme for the plantation of Ireland would diminish the number of soldiers required to hold the country, and before the end of July the assent of the chiefs of the army in England having been obtained, the Council also sanctioned not merely a sweeping reduction in the strength of the regiments in Great Britain, but a diminution of the amount of the pay both of officers and soldiers. Once more Oliver had acted in accordance with the Instrument, and with the wishes of the dissolved Parliament. The £60,000 a month which Parliament had thought sufficient for the assessment was not exceeded, whilst the army was reduced at least approximately to the numbers accepted alike by Parliament and the Instrument. It might be hard to give a satisfactory answer to those who denied the validity of the Instrument; but, if this validity were acknowledged, it would be equally hard to refute those who argued that Oliver was doing his best to rule as a constitutional magistrate.

Would it be possible for Oliver to persist in this attitude to the end, in spite of the growing demands on the exchequer? In March, 1655, Penruddock's rising had extracted from Oliver an order for the calling out and organisation of the militia, which was, however, countermanded upon the prompt repression of the insurrection. In May, however, the officers who recommended the reduction of the army, also recommended the establishment of a militia for purposes of police, and as the summer advanced and the information which came in from Thurloe's spies announced that the Royalist plots were by no means at an end, this plan assumed greater consistency. The scheme of appointing a militia-police had at least this to be said in its favour, that the proposal had been favoured by Parliament. If Parliament had been allowed to work out its own scheme, it would probably have subjected the militia to local officers, and provided for its wants by local payments. Oliver took care to bring it into disciplinary connection with the army, by placing it under eleven Major-Generals. Taxation for its support he could not demand without infringing on the Instrument. In his perplexity he, or one of his advisers, hit upon a plan for raising supplies from the Royalists alone, who were called on to contribute a tenth of their income for the purpose. It was their refusal to submit peaceably to a settled Government which had caused the difficulty, and it was for them to bear the expense of the measures which had been necessitated by their misconduct. Such an exaction, being no general taxation, might be considered by interested parties as saving the authority of the Instrument. Of any sympathetic feeling with the Royalists whose property had been diminished by past confiscations, and whose political and religious ideals had been thrown to the ground, there was, it is needless to say, nothing in Oliver's mind. They were but enemies to be crushed, or at least to be reduced to impotence.

That the Royalists had religious ideals of their own was a provocation which made it easy to deny them the toleration which they had hitherto virtually enjoyed. The familiar cadences of the Book of Common Prayer had become to them a symbol of political as well as of religious faith, whilst the voice of the often long-winded, and sometimes irrelevant ejaculator of prayers of his own conception, stood for them as the embodiment of the forces which had conspired to murder their king, to deprive them of the broad acres sold to satisfy the demands of sequestrators, and to exclude them from all share in the public interests of the country which they loved as devotedly as any Puritan could possibly do. It was now that Oliver committed the mistake—which thousands of others in like circumstances have committed—of confounding the symbol with the cause. The use of the Common Prayer Book was proscribed as thoroughly as the mass. Noblemen and gentlemen were prohibited from entertaining the ejected clergy of their own Church as chaplains or tutors of their children. Yet, after all, the persecution was sharp only for a time, and not only was the inquisition into the religious practices of domestic life soon abandoned, but the Episcopalian clergy were led to understand that no harm should befall them so long as they abstained from thrusting themselves upon the notice of the public.

It was not only in relation to religious toleration that Oliver was driven by his position to modify his earlier principles. At one time he had fully sympathised with the Independent party in its efforts to secure the liberty of the press. Of libels on his own character and person he had been widely tolerant. Step by step the Long Parliament had imposed restrictions on the press, and these restrictions were continued under the Protectorate. At last, in October, 1655, the final blow fell. Only two weekly newspapers were permitted to appear, and both these newspaper were to be edited by an agent of the Government. Milton, now incapacitated by blindness from active employment in the service of the State, must have winced at hearing that his chosen hero, who had long ago turned his back on a voluntary system of Church-government, had now turned his back on the central doctrine of the Areopagitica. Oliver, we may be sure, took all these proceedings as a matter of course. He held himself to have been placed in the seat of authority not to advance the most beneficent theories, but to keep order after the fashion of a constable in a discordant world. Neither Milton nor himself believed in the political rights of majorities. If the nation chose to raise itself up against the cause of God, so much the worse for the nation. "I say," he had announced to his first Parliament, "that the wilful throwing away of this Government—so owned by God, so approved by men, so testified to in the fundamentals of it—and that in relation to the good of these nations and posterity; I can sooner be willing to be rolled into my grave and buried with infamy, than I can give my consent unto." Oliver doubtless held that the partitioning of England into eleven districts, each under a military chief, was consistent with at least a literal observance of "this Government," as he himself had called it.

It is possible that if the Major-Generals had confined themselves to keeping watch over the Royalist gentry, with occasionally breaking up their religious meetings, and with driving away the chaplains and the tutors of their sons, they would have caused less irritation than they did. The army, however, or in plainer terms, the occupants of its higher posts, from the Lord Protector downwards, were the most systematic upholders of that aggressive Puritan morality, which was diluted with greater worldliness in other circles. It is no doubt untrue that Justices of the Peace, as has sometimes been suggested, were altogether inefficient during the Protectorate; but they were not loved by the Cavalier gentry, whose estates were often larger than their own; and, like all local authorities, they were hampered by the local feeling which, even amongst those who willingly accepted the Protectorate, was, though certainly not Episcopalian, far from being as acutely Puritan as was desired at head-quarters. A statute inflicting the penalty of death upon adulterers had been reduced almost to a dead letter by the unwillingness of juries to convict; and—to take an instance from the daily amusements of the people—the bear-garden at Southwark had survived the prohibition of one Puritan Government after another, till, a few weeks after the appointment of the Major-Generals, Pride, who had once blocked the doors of Parliament, slew the bears with his own hands, and closed the exhibition.

As to the Major-Generals themselves, they were soon instructed to tighten the reins of discipline, co-operating with willing and spurring unwilling magistrates to suppress not merely treason and rebellion, but vice and immorality. Their orders were to put down horse-racing, cock-fighting and other sports which brought together crowds of doubtful fidelity to the government. They were told to promote godliness and virtue, and to see to the execution of the laws against drunkenness, blasphemy, swearing, play-acting, profanation of the Lord's Day, and so forth; and also to put down gaming-houses in Westminster and ale-houses in the country, lest evil and factious men should congregate in them. They were to keep an open eye on the beneficed clergy, calling for the ejection of those who either showed tendencies favourable to the Book of Common Prayer, or brought disgrace by laxity of conduct on the Puritanism they professed. During the first six or nine months of 1656, when these men ruled supreme, the anti-Puritan fervour which was before long to lay low both the Protectorate and the Commonwealth, ceased to be the special note of particular classes and rooted itself in general society, far outside the circle of ordinary royalism.

Chapter 6

A Parliamentary Constitution

IT WAS all the worse for Oliver from the financial point of view, that he was now pursuing a foreign policy which—whatever opinion we may have of it on other grounds—at least increased the burdens of the nation to a point at which Englishmen began to grow restive. Even before the signature of the Dutch peace in the spring of 1654, Oliver had cast about in his mind for a foreign policy, and it was only on rare occasions that he appears to have contemplated the possibility of keeping peace with all nations unless he were compelled to engage in war in defence of the honour or interests of the country. He seemed to have regarded the victorious fleet bequeathed to him by the Commonwealth and the victorious army which he had done more than any other man to forge into an instrument of dominion, as inviting him to choose an enemy to be the object of his defiance, rather than sure guards for the country which he ruled. The sword itself drew on the man, and the weakness of the two great Continental nations, France and Spain, embroiled in an internecine war, each coveting the alliance of England, and each dreading her enmity, increased its attractive power.

Not that Oliver was without principles underlying his actions. He had indeed two—not always easily reconcilable. He wanted to increase the trade of the country by strengthening its maritime power, and he wanted to uphold the cause of God in Europe by the formation of a great Protestant alliance against what he believed to be the aggressive Papacy. This second principle gave to his actions a nobility which only an honest devotion to higher than material interests can impart, whilst at the same time it led him into the greatest practical mistakes of his career, because he was always ready to overestimate the persecuting tendencies of the Roman Catholic States, which, since the Peace of Westphalia, had been local and spasmodic, and to overestimate the strength of religious conviction in the rulers of Protestant States, as well as to imagine it possible to unite these last in a Protestant crusade. It was a still more deplorable result that his own character became somewhat deteriorated by the constant effort to persuade himself that he was following the higher motives, when in reality material considerations weighed most heavily in the scale.

In truth, Oliver's day of rule lay between two worlds—the world in which the existence of Protestantism had been really at stake, at the time when men so alien from the dogmatism of the sects as Drake, Raleigh and Sidney had enlisted in its cause—and the world of trade and manufacture, which was springing into being. Oliver's mind comprehended both. Doubtless his mind was the roomier that it could respond to the double current, but it was not to be expected that a generation whose face was set in the direction of material interests should be otherwise than impatient of a call to the Heavens to place themselves on the side of English trade.

During the greater part of 1654 Oliver had been hesitating whether to ally himself with Spain or with France. For some time he inclined to the side of Spain. His religious sympathies were touched by the sufferings of the French Huguenots. The succour which he proposed to convey to them would have brought him into direct alliance with Spain, and it was only the revelation of Spanish financial and military weakness which turned him aside from his project. Then came a suggestion long weighed and finally taken up, for carrying on war against the Spanish West Indies. It would be hard to deny that, even in modern eyes, a *casus belli,* apart from all ideal schemes of weakening the Government which sheltered the Inquisition, was to be found—not in the refusal of the Spanish authorities to allow English ships to trade in the Spanish islands, but in the deliberate seizure of English ships and the enslavement of English crews guilty of no other crime than that of being bound for Barbados or for some other English colony. The strangest part of the matter is that Oliver closed his eyes to the natural consequence of an attack upon a Spanish colony. He fancied that it would be still possible to carry out the Elizabethan plan of keeping peace in Europe and making war in the Indies. He was probably strengthened in this opinion by the fact that, almost from the first days of the Commonwealth, a war of reprisals had been going on at sea with France without disturbing the nominally amicable relations between the two countries. Why should he not take a West Indian Island as a reprisal for the seizure of English ships, and peace be maintained with Spain as if nothing had happened?

Before the end of 1654 two fleets sailed on their several missions. The one, under Blake, entered the Mediterranean, where he was most hospitably received by the Governors of the Spanish ports and by the officials of the Grand Duke of Tuscany at Leghorn. He ransomed a number of English captives at Algiers, but the Bey of Tunis, some of whose subjects had recently been sold for galley-slaves to the Knights of Malta by an English scoundrel, was naturally less compliant. Blake destroyed nine of his vessels at Porto Farina, but Tunis itself was inaccessible, and he was unable to recover a single English slave from that quarter. Penn sailed for Barbados with some 2,500 soldiers on board under Venables. Both in Barbados and in other English islands reinforcements were shipped, and with this ill-compounded force a landing was effected in Hispaniola. The attempt to seize on the city of San Domingo failed, and the expedition sailed for Jamaica, at that time little more than a desert island, and established itself in possession. Some years passed before the colony became self-supporting, but Oliver was unremitting in his resolution not only to increase the numbers of the first military settlers, but to supply them with all things necessary for the foundation of homes in the wilderness. It was annoying that the first operations in the Spanish West Indies had opened with a check, but it was doubtless fortunate that the new English colony was not built up on Spanish foundations. The soldiers who, on their march towards San Domingo, pelted with oranges an image of the Virgin which they had torn down from the walls of a deserted monastery, would hardly have been at their best in the midst of a Roman Catholic population.

Much to Oliver's surprise, the news of the proceedings of his men in Hispaniola aroused the bitterest indignation at Madrid, an indignation already, to some extent, aroused when Blake sailed out through the Straits of Gibraltar to meet and capture the treasure ships expected from America. The features of Philip IV as—thanks to the brush of Velasquez—they meet us in every noted gallery in Europe, are not those of a man remarkable for wisdom, but he had none of the lingering hesitancy of his grandfather, Philip II. He ordered the seizure of the property of English merchants in Spanish harbours; and Oliver, after balancing for two years between France and Spain, had the question decided by his own mistaken belief that the world of Elizabeth remained unchanged. The breach with Spain necessitated a reconsideration of the relations between England and France. Ever since his accession to the Protectorate, Oliver had evaded the demands of the French Ambassador, Bordeaux, for a cessation of the war of reprisals at sea which had been bequeathed him by the Commonwealth. As English privateers captured more prizes than those of the French, he was in no hurry to bring the situation to an end till he obtained of Mazarin, the virtual ruler of France, a tacit understanding that the Huguenots should no longer be maltreated, and an express undertaking to expel from France the English Royal family and the chief Royalists in attendance on the exiled Court. Whilst these questions were still under discussion, an event occurred which, more than any other single action in his life, brought into relief the higher side of Cromwell's character and policy. In January, 1655, the young Duke of Savoy—or rather his mother, who, though he had come to years of discretion, acted in his name—ordered that the Vaudois, whose religion, though now akin to the Protestantism of the seventeenth century, dated from mediæval times, should be removed from the plain at the foot of the Piedmontese Valleys into which they had spread, to the upper and barer reaches, on the pretext that they had broken the bounds assigned them by his ancestors. In April his troops entered the valley, slaying and torturing as they went. When the news reached England in May, Oliver's heart was moved to its depths. He ordered a day of humiliation to be held, and a house-to-house visitation to collect money for the sufferers. Upward of £38,000 was gathered in the end, the Protector heading the list with £2,000. He sent a Minister to Turin to remonstrate, but his warmest appeals were addressed to Mazarin, the all-powerful Minister of Louis XIV, as some French troops, acting as allies of the Duke in his war against the Spaniards in Italy, had been concerned in the massacre. Mazarin was plainly told that there would be no treaty with France till these massacres were stopped. The French Minister had been so long deluded of his hope of a treaty that this threat alone might not have terrified him, but he feared that Oliver would hire the Protestant Swiss to take part against the Duke of Savoy, and that all thought of fighting the Spaniards in Italy would have to be laid aside for that year. Communications passed between Paris and Turin, and the Duke of Savoy issued his pardon—such was the term employed—to the surviving Vaudois.

Milton's sonnet marks well this highest point of the Protector's action upon Continental States:—

> Avenge, O Lord, thy slaughtered saints, whose bones
> Lie scattered on the Alpine mountains cold;
> Even them who kept thy truth so pure of old,
> When all our fathers worshipped stocks and stones
> Forget not: in thy book record their groans
> Who were thy sheep, and in their ancient fold
> Slain by the bloody Piedmontese, that rolled
> Mother with infant down the rocks. Their moans
> The vales redoubled to the hills, and they
> To heaven. Their martyred blood and ashes sow
> O'er all the Italian fields, where still doth sway

The triple Tyrant; that from these may grow
A hundred fold, who having learnt thy way
Early may fly the Babylonian woe.

In championing the Vaudois, Oliver's Puritanism had served the noblest interests of humanity. With somewhat of the poet's fervour Milton saw in the defence of the oppressed victims of the Duke of Savoy a challenge to the spiritual tyranny of Papal Rome. It made Oliver, we may be sure, more ready to take up the challenge of Spain, and to come to terms with the French Government which had spoken on the side of tolerance. Yet, enthusiastically Puritan as he was, he could not deal with the external affairs of England from a merely or even a mainly religious point of view. His position would not allow it—nor his character. The mingling of spirirtual with worldly motives might produce strange results. At one time it elevated and ennobled action. At another time the two motives might clash together, the one frustrating the other. In the stand taken by Oliver on behalf of the Vaudois, the spiritual had predominated over the material aim. In the breach with Spain, his belief in the predominance of the religious motive burnt strongly in Oliver's own mind: it was less conspicuous to onlookers.

The first result of the quarrel between England and Spain was the conclusion of a commerical treaty with France, which put an end to the war of reprisals which had now lasted more than six years. All question of a closer alliance was reserved, perhaps rather because it demanded time for consideration than because there was any doubt in Oliver's mind as to his intention in the matter. Before the war had been far prolonged the exiled King took refuge in the Spanish Netherlands, holding close communication with Englishmen who plotted the destruction of the Protector, whilst privateers issuing from Dunkirk and Ostend preyed upon English commerce and irritated the London merchants who had no enthusiasm for a religious war, and who regretted the loss of their goods seized in Spanish ports. In the spring and summer of 1656 the necessity of doing something against an active enemy established so near the English coast would have driven Oliver into the arms of France even if he had not already contemplated such an alliance. Yet it was during these very months that the desired end seemed to be eluding his grasp. Mazarin, unwilling to allow an English garrison to occupy Dunkirk as the price of the Protector's alliance, was doing his best to come to terms with Spain, which would have enabled him to dispense with English aid. It was not till the approach of autumn that the French Minister, discovering that his overtures to Philip IV had been made in vain, bowed to the inevitable, and agreed to hand over Dunkirk to England, if it could be wrested from Spain by the united effort of the two countries. What a vista was opened up of vast military and naval expenditure by the mere enunciation of such a project! The reduction of the army in the summer of 1655 could hardly be maintained under these altered circumstances; and with an increased army and navy, what chance was there for that government according to the Instrument which had been the corner-stone of Oliver's domestic policy?

The difficulty was the greater because in the summer of 1656 it appeared that the plan of policing the country by a militia under Major-Generals had broken down financially. Meetings of officers were summoned in June to discuss the situation, and though the Protector was at first inclined to raise fresh taxation on his own sole authority, he soon recognised that such a step would be too unpopular to meet with success, and resolved that another Parliament must be summoned. Before the new Parliament met, Oliver had recourse to one of those startling privileges which the Instrument might be quoted as having conferred on his Government. That constitution assigned to the Council the right of examining and rejecting such members as might be elected without possessing the qualifications imposed by it on members of Parliament, a right which the Council now exercised in the rejection of at least ninety-three hostile members. In the case of Royalists chosen by constituencies the Council was undoubtedly in the right in annulling their elections, at least so far as the constitution was concerned. In refusing admission to Republicans like Scott and Hazlerigg it was compelled to have recourse to a quibble. It was true that the Council was empowered by the Instrument to reject members who were not "of known integrity." That body with at least the tacit approval of the Protector now interpreted those words as giving them power to reject members not of known integrity to the existing constitution. For once in his life Oliver demeaned himself to act in the spirit of a pettifogging attorney. Base as the action was, it was only possible because the greater number of those admitted to their seats, whether through the pressure put upon the country by the Major-Generals, or because they looked with more hopefulness to the Protector, were now prepared to give him their support. In the speech with which Oliver opened the session on September 17, he did his best to rouse the indignation of his hearers against Spain. "Why, truly," he urged, "your great enemy is the Spaniard. He is a natural enemy. He is naturally so; he is naturally so throughout—by reason of that enmity that is in him against whatsoever is of God." It was the keynote of Oliver's feeling in this matter in his more exalted mood. His sentiments as a patriotic Englishman found vent in a long catalogue of wrongs suffered at the hands of Spaniards from Elizabeth's time to his own. His defiance of Spain was followed by an attack on Charles Stuart,—now dwelling on Spanish soil, and hopefully looking to Spain for troops to replace him on the throne—in which he referred to him as "a captain to lead us back into Egypt." Then came a retrospect on the Cavalier plots and a justification of the Major-Generals, who had been established to repress them. The war with Spain must be prosecuted vigorously—in other words, money must be voted to maintain the struggle at home and abroad. Oliver's speech did not all turn upon what ordinary men term politics. "Make it a shame," he cried, "to see men bold in sin and profaneness, and God will bless you. You will be a blessing to the nation; and by this will be more repairers of breaches than by anything in the world. Truly these things do respect the souls of men, and the spirits—which are the men. The mind is the man. If that be kept pure, a man signifies somewhat; if not, I would very fain see what difference there is betwixt him and a beast. He hath only some activity to do some more mischief." It was the voice of the higher—because more universal—Puritanism which rang in these words, a voice which soared to worlds above the region of ceremonial form or doctrinal dispute, echoing, as from the lips of a man of practical wrestlings with the world, the voice of the imaginative poet who, in the days of his youth, had taught that

> So dear to Heaven is saintly chastity
> That, when a soul is found sincerely so,
> A thousand liveried angels lackey her,
> Driving far off each thing of sin and guilt,
> And in clear dream and solemn vision
> Tell her of things that no gross ear can hear,
> Till oft converse with heavenly habitants
> Begin to cast a beam on the outward shape,
> The unpolluted temple of the mind,
> And turns it by degrees to the soul's essence
> Till all be made immortal.

Oliver had to touch earth again with a financial statement and to crave for Parliamentary supplies. A demand for money was not particularly welcome to the members, and they preferred to wrangle for some weeks over the case of James Naylor, a fanatic who had allowed himself to be greeted as the Messiah by his feminine admirers. In October news came that Stayner, in command of a detachment from Blake's fleet, had destroyed or captured a part of the Plate Fleet off the Spanish coast, and in the following month the carts were rolling through the London streets on their way to the Tower with silver worth £200,000. Emboldened by this success, Oliver's confidants brought in a bill perpetuating the decimation of the Royalists by act of Parliament. The bill was rejected, and hard words were spoken of the Major-Generals. Oliver accepted the decision of the House, and the Major-Generals were withdrawn.

There is good reason to believe that Oliver consented willingly to the vote. He was never one to persist in methods once adopted, if he could obtain his larger aims in some other way. The debates had revealed that the House was divided into two parties, a minority clinging to the army as a political force, and a majority calling for the establishment of the government on a civil basis. The latter was even more devoted to the Protector than the former, and Oliver, who in his heart concurred with their views, was prepared, as indeed he had been prepared in 1654, to submit the Instrument to revision. The difference was that he was assured now —as he had not been assured then—that Parliament would sustain the fundamental principles which he regarded as the most precious part of the constitution.

In January, 1657, a fresh attempt to assassinate the Protector—this time by Miles Sindercombe—gave reason, or perhaps excuse, for loyal demonstrations, and a month later the House entered upon the discussion of a proposal for a constitutional revision, ultimately known as *The Humble Petition and Advice*, of which the article which attracted the most general attention was that which reconstituted the Kingship in the person of Oliver, with the power of nominating his own successor. The demand for the revival of the Kingship was no mere work of zealous flatterers. The crown was held in the House to be the symbol of civilian as opposed to military government, but for this reason the offer of it was assailed by the leading officers, headed by Lambert who, in 1653, had offered the crown to the man to whom he now refused it. So far as the officers were concerned, they appear to have been actuated, in part at least, by a dread that a Parliamentary Protectorate would in the end turn out to be other than a Puritan Protectorate. Lambert's own motives were somewhat more difficult to unravel. Possibly he regarded a Kingship by the grace of Parliament less of a boon than a Kingship by the grace of the army. Still more probably was he moved by a personal grievance in seeing Fleetwood, who had now returned from Ireland, higher than himself in the favour of the Protector, perhaps even in the favour of the army. In any case he carried on the campaign with consummate skill, keeping aloof from the constitutional question and throwing all his strength into the argument—which the rudest soldier could understand—that the army had not rejected one king in order to set up another. When he won over Fleetwood and Desborough, the son-in-law and brother-in-law of the Protector, to his side, he had practically won the game, especially as he was able to back a petition against a revival of the Royal title by the subscription of a hundred officers. Oliver kept up the negotiation with Parliament as long as he could, but in the end he refused the crown offered to him rather than alienate the army. The remaining articles of *The Humble Petition and Advice* were then agreed to, and on June 26 Oliver was solemnly installed as Protector, under a Parliamentary title, with all but Royal pomp at Westminster Hall.

Too much has been made by some modern writers of Oliver's defeat on the question of the Kingship. The title, as he himself truly said, would have been but a feather in his cap. It is doubtful whether its acceptance would have disarmed a single enemy. The rocks upon which the Protector was running were of a far too substantial character to be removed by the assumption of an ill-fitting symbol. Whether he wore a crown or not, no one could have regarded Oliver as Charles I had been regarded; or even as William III, who in some sort continued the Protector's work, came afterwards to be regarded.

Apart from the really unimportant question of the crown, the military party had for the time been beaten all along the line. Not only had the Major-Generals disappeared, and Lambert himself, driven to surrender all his offices, military or civil, retired to the cultivation of tulips at Wimbledon; but *The Humble Petition and Advice,* that is to say, a Parliamentary constitution, had entirely displaced the Instrument of government as the fundamental law of the three nations. The more important of the stipulations of the new constitution were necessarily of the nature of a compromise. In return for the establishment of a second House composed of his own nominees, the Protector was able to abandon the claim of the Council to exclude members of what must now be regarded as the House of Commons—seeing that a vote with which he was dissatisfied would be of no avail if it was no more than the vote of a single House. Nor was it only an occasional check on the old House that he had gained.

The new House, nominated by himself in the first place, was endowed with the right in the future of excluding from its benches any new member nominated by himself or by a future Protector. As he took care to name none who were not strong Puritans and devoted to the Protectorate, he expected that the new House would be able, for all time, to reject legislation contrary to the interests of Puritanism or to the Protectoral constitution. The question of finance, which had wrecked the last Parliament, was settled in a way equally satisfactory to the Protector. The number of soldiers to be kept on foot was passed over in silence, whilst the same sum, £1,800,000, which had been approved by the first Protectorate Parliament as needful for the wants of the army and navy together with those of the domestic government, was now granted, not for five years as had been proposed by the former Parliament, but till the Protector and the two Houses agreed to alter it. The scheme by which the Instrument had fixed the strength of the army at 30,000 men, and had then left the Protector and Council free to levy whatever supplies they thought needful for its support, was deliberately left out of account. On paper, the terms of agreement showed fairly enough. England had at last got a constitution which was no production of a military coterie. Protector and Parliament were at last at one. Unfortunately, those who had welcomed this fair concord took little account of the forces which were likely to govern events in the not far distant future—the force of the army, whose handiwork had been set at nought—the force of the Parliamentary tradition strengthened by the work of the Long Parliament—and, above all, the force of discontent with the shifting sands on which the new Government was built, a discontent which might easily show itself in a national call for the restoration of the Stuart King—not because his person was loved, but because he would bring with him what appeared to be the strong basis of old use and wont.

Oliver was not wholly absorbed in constitutional struggles or in foreign conflicts. In administration his Government stands supreme above all which had preceded it, because no other ruler united so wide a tolerance of divergencies of opinion with so keen an eye for individual merit. He could gather round him the enthusiastic Milton to pen those dignified State Papers in which he announced his resolutions to the Powers of Europe; Andrew Marvell, the most transparently honest of men, who, with all his admiration for Oliver, had mingled in the verses written by him as a panegyric on his patron those lines recording Charles's dignified appearance on the scaffold, which will be remembered when all his other writings in prose or verse are forgotten. In Oliver's Council sat Bulstrode Whitelocke, the somewhat stolid lawyer, who, too cautious to give a precedent approval to Oliver's revolutionary acts, was always ready to acccept the situation created by them, and yet sufficiently inspired by professional feeling to resign his post as Commissioner of the Great Seal rather than accept the Protector's reforms in the Court of Chancery. There too sat Nathaniel Fiennes, the second son of Lord Saye and Sele, not indeed a statesman with broad views, but ready at any moment to pen State Papers in defence of a Government which had rescued him from the neglect into which he had fallen—probably undeservedly—in consequence of his hasty surrender of Bristol in the Civil War. Amongst Oliver's diplomatists were Morland and Lockhart. Amongst his admirals, the honoured Blake and the ever-faithful Montague. Amongst those who at one time or another were his chaplains were Owen, the ecclesiastical statesman, and Howe, whose exemplary piety led him to doubt whether the Protector's household was sufficiently religious, and whose broad-minded charity prepared him to abandon the Church of the Restoration, not because it was un-Puritan, but because it was exclusive.

Yet, after all is said, the list of ancient allies driven by the Protector from public life, and in some cases actually deprived of liberty, was even more note-worthy. The most placable of men could hardly have avoided a quarrel with John Lilburne, of whom it was said that if he alone were left alive in the world, John would dispute with Lilburne and Lilburne with John; but it is at least remarkable that under Oliver's sway Vane, whom he had long dealt with as a brother; Harrison, who had fought under him from the very beginning of the

Civil War, and who had stood by his side when the members of the Long Parliament were thrust out of doors; Hazlerigg, who had kept guard over the English border in the crisis of Dunbar; Okey, who had led the dragoons at Naseby; Overton, the trusted Governor of Hull, next to London the most important military post in England; Lambert, who had taken a foremost part in the preparation of the Instrument of Government; Cooper, who had been one of his most trusted councillors—to say nothing of confidants of less conspicuous note—were either in prison or in disgrace. When the second Protectorate, as it is sometimes called, was launched on its course, the only man not connected with the family of the Protector, who still occupied anything like an independent position, was Monk, the Governor and Commander-in-Chief in Scotland, and it is probable that he owed his authority to the distance which kept him from interfering in English politics. The true explanation appears to be that the men from whom Oliver parted were men not merely of definite principles, but of definite ideas. Each one had made up his mind that England was to be served by the establishment of some particular form of government, or some particular course of action. Oliver's mind was certainly not without the guidance of definite principles. He could not conceive it to be right to abandon religion to men who, whether Episcopalian or Presbyterian, would impose fetters on the freedom of "the people of God." He could not admit the claim of an hereditary monarch or of an elected Parliament to decide against the best interests of the country. Within these limits, however, his mind was more elastic than those of his opponents. Steadied by his high aims, he could vary the methods with which he combated each evil of the day as it arose. Those who attached themselves to him in his struggle against the King or against the different Parliaments of his time, or against the military power, were as incapable as he was capable of facing round to confront each new danger as it arose. From the moment that each partial victory was won, the old friends had to be reasoned with, then discarded, and at last restrained from doing mischief. As years went on, Oliver, in spite of the abilities of those still serving under him, became increasingly an isolated man. Not only did his strong sense of religion in its Puritan form alienate those who were not Puritans or not religious, but his frequent changes of attitude bewildered that easy-going mass of mankind which sticks to its own theory, more especially if its own interests are embodied in it, and regards all change of political method as a veil intended to conceal moral turpitude. Oliver had decidedly lost adherents since the establishment of the Protectorate.

It was probably the increasing sense of the untrustworthiness of political support, rather than nepotism in its ordinary sense, which led the Protector to rely more and more on the services of members of his own family. His younger son, Henry Cromwell, was now Lord Deputy of Ireland. His son-in-law, Fleetwood, was not only a member of the Council, but, now that Lambert was in disgrace, the most influential officer in the army, marked out for its command if Oliver were to pass away. His brother-in-law, Desborough, occupied a position hardly inferior. Two other brothers-in-law, Colonel John Jones and Colonel Valentine Wauton, were members of the Council in England or Ireland. Lockhart, one of the few Scotchmen who had rallied to the Protectorate, and who was engaged as a diplomatist in riveting the bonds between France and England, took to wife the Protector's niece. A son-in-law, John Claypole, was now Master of the Horse. In the army, Whalley and Ingoldsby were his cousins. Not one of these, however, failed to occupy with credit the position he had acquired, whilst Oliver's reluctance to push forward Richard, the elder of his surviving sons, may be taken as evidence that his affection for his family did not override his devotion to the State. Richard's tastes lay in the direction of dogs and horses. He had recently broken his leg, hunting in the New Forest, and, upon his recovery, was brought up to Westminster to assume his place, on the establishment of the second Protectorate. Before that time, only two of the Councillors not holding other office, Lambert and Strickland, hand received the title of "Lord," probably having it verbally conferred upon them, and certainly not, as has been sometimes said, in connection with any Household appointment.

Officials of high rank had—like the Lord Deputy and the Lord Keeper of the old monarchy—been entitled Lords, as in the case of Whitelocke, now Lord Commissioner of the Treasury, and Fiennes, Lord Commissioner of the Great Seal. Gradually usage, quickly sanctioned by official notice, gave the title of Lord to the Protector's sons and sons-in-law, and of Lady to his daughters. The Lord Richard was only admitted to the Council on the last day of 1657, and was treated with some of the observances due to the heir, but till the last his father held back from exercising that power of nominating a successor which had been conferred on him by the latest constitution.

So far as in him lay, Oliver took care that his family should be an example to all the families in the land. Strict as he was in banishing not merely vice, but the folly that leads to vice, he was no more opposed to reasonable amusement than other more sober Puritans of the day. Music and song had a special charm for him, and amongst his soldiers he showed his appreciation of a healthy jest, laughing heartily, for instance, on his way to the campaign of Dunbar, when one of them slammed an overturned cream-tub on the head of another. After the victory at Worcester he was heard of in a hawking party near Aylesbury, and if he prohibited horse-races, together with the drama, cock-fights and bear-baitings, it was not because he disliked amusement, but partly because he set himself against the immorality with which these particular amusements were accompanied, and partly because the confluence of spectators concealed the assembling of Royalist and other conspirators. Of horses he was quite as good a judge as his son Richard, and it was from a spirited pair of runaway steeds which had been given to him by the Count of Oldenburg that he nearly met his death in the early days of the Protectorate. Of late years Oliver's enjoyment of country life had been much curtailed. Other rulers had been in the habit of making summer progresses which took them away from business and the life of towns. Oliver—if he invented nothing else—may be regarded as the inventor of that modified form or enjoyment to which hard-working citizens have, in our day, given the name of the "week-end." Liable to assault on every hand, he did not venture to leave the seat of Government for long, and he found repose in a weekly visit to Hampton Court, which lasted from Saturday to Monday, the length of his sojourn being only rarely extended by illness or some unusual family occurrence.

The domestic life of the Protector was all that might be expected from a man whose heart was as warm as his spirit was high. In the midst of his most arduous labours he seldom passed a day, as long as he was at Whitehall, on which he did not dine and sup in the family circle, and up till his aged mother's death in 1654 he was in the habit of visiting her every night before she retired to rest. Of his four daughters two were already married, the eldest, Bridget, after the death of her first husband, Ireton, having become the wife of Fleetwood; and the second, the sprightly and graceful Elizabeth, had married John, otherwise Lord Claypole, whom the Protector had entrusted with the charge of his stables, under the style of Master of the Horse. On November 11, 1657, some months after the commencement of the second Protectorate, Frances, the youngest of the four, was married to Robert Rich, the grandson of the Earl of Warwick, the Lord High Admiral of the Long Parliament, and in the following week her sister Mary was married to Lord Fauconberg. The first of these two marriages was long delayed by the Protector's doubts as to the character of the suitor, as well as by his dissatisfaction with the proposed settlement—Oliver's moral sense once more entwining itself with his practical decisions. It was said at the time that he valued the Fauconberg alliance more than that with the Warwick family, as winning over a Royalist peer to his side.

Not one of Oliver's four daughter ever gave their father cause for real anxiety. Though they were less strenuous than himself and sometimes needed, in his judgment, to be spurred on to higher spiritual aims, he never seems to have addressed them otherwise than as those who were worthy of parental love. If he really preferred Lady Claypole to his other daughters, it was most likely because she was more sprightly and less outwardly pious than her sisters. "Your sister Claypole," he had written to Bridget soon after she had become Ireton's wife, "is, I trust in mercy, exercised with some perplexed thoughts. She sees her own vanity and carnal mind; bewailing it. She seeks after—as I hope also—what will satisfy: and thus to be a seeker is to be of the best sect next to a finder; and such an one shall every faithful humble seeker be at the end. Happy seeker, happy finder! Who ever tasted that the Lord is gracious, without some sense of self, vanity, and badness? Who ever tasted that graciousness of His, and could go less in desire—less than pressing after full enjoyment?" Of Bridget herself he writes with fuller assurance. "Dear Heart," he continues, "press on; let no husband, let not anything cool thy affections after Christ. I hope he will be an occasion to inflame them. That which is best worthy of love in thy husband is that of the image of Christ he bears. Look on that, and love it best, and all the rest for that. I pray for thee and him; do so for me." Yet even Bridget was far from answering to the modern conception of the Puritan lady, as is testified by the splendid yellow silk petticoat which has been handed down from generation to generation in the family of her eldest daughter. Nevertheless it was not Bridget's vanity which was most on her father's mind. Five years later, in writing to his wife from Edinburgh, he begs her to "mind poor Betty," *i.e.* Elizabeth, Lady Claypole, "of the Lord's great mercy," and to urge her to "take heed of a departing heart and of being cozened with worldly vanities and worldly company, which I doubt she is too subject to." The liveliness which cause such searchings of heart was doubtless the tie which bound more firmly Oliver's love to her. One day we hear of her demurely assuring Whitelocke that it was fear of his great influence which had caused her father to send him out of the way to Sweden when he was about to assume the Protectorate. At another time we are told of her driving with her cousin Ingoldsby and two of her sisters, all the three ladies dressed in green, whilst the courtier-like crowd watch their movements and bow as they pass. Then we hear of the scornful language in which, with the pride of a lady by birth as well as by her father's advancement, she accounted for the absence of the wives of some of the Major-Generals from an entertainment at which she took part: "I warrant you they are washing their dishes at home as they used to do." Yet withal she had an open ear for trouble, and a ready tongue to plead not in vain the cause of the innocent with her father. By the summer of 1657 her health had been failing, and at one time her life had been despaired of.

Oliver's own health was far from being such as to promise length of days. Though he had had no serious illness since the time when his life was in danger in Scotland after the toils and anxiety of the Dunbar compaign, short spells of ill-health are frequently mentioned, and the Venetian Ambassador, presented to him in the autumn of 1655, noticed the shaking hand with which he held his hat in welcoming him, a symptom of weakness which left its mark on his hand-writing during the later period of his life. In the summer of 1657 he was detained at Hampton Court by illness, apparently of the character of malarial fever, for more than a week. Yet his spirit was as high, his resolution as strong as ever. At no time had the state of public affairs made larger demand upon his mental powers than in the last fourteen months of his life. It is true that the adoption of the new Parliamentary constitution had appeared for a moment to have solved the problem of domestic government, but his sagacity would have been far less than it was if he had imagined that all his difficulties were at an end.

If, on the other hand, the Protector looked abroad, fortune appeared to smile. Whilst Parliament was still in session, news arrived that Blake had destroyed the Spanish treasure fleet under the protection of forts in the harbour of Santa Cruz in Teneriffe. It was the most hazardous, and consequently the most glorious action of a noble and patriotic life. Worn out by toils and exposure, Blake sought and obtained leave to come home in search of the rest he so sorely needed. Before the vessel that bore him reached Plymouth his spirit had passed away. The great admiral was honoured with a public funeral in Westminster Abbey.

Spain, with her supply of treasure from the Indies cut short, was incapacitated from serious warlike effort, and already the alliance was forged which was to force her into submission. Even before the victory was won at Santa Cruz a treaty had been signed between Oliver and Louis XIV, arranging for a joint attack on the Spanish fortresses of Dunkirk, Mardyke and Gravelines, the first two to fall to the share of England, the last to that of France. An English force of 6,000 men was to be combined with a French force of 20,000, the blockade at sea being entrusted to an English fleet. Half the English contingent was at once despatched under Sir John Reynolds, but either the necessities of war, or the reluctance of Mazarin to carry out his engagements, led him to prefer the distant siege of Montmédy to an attack on the coast towns, and it was only after a warm expostulation from the Protector that measures were taken to carry out the treaty. Of the quality of the English contingent there could be no doubt. Turenne—whose praise in military matters was praise indeed—declared that he had never seen finer troops. As soon as Mazarin was found to be in earnest, the remaining 3,000 men were despatched to Flanders, and before the end of October Mardyke was captured and loyally placed in the hands of an English garrison. Farther than this it was impossible to go at so advanced a season. In the summer of 1658, the combined armies defeated the Spaniards on the Dunes, and Dunkirk itself was added to the possessions of England on the Continent.

The wisdom of a foreign policy which gave England a land-frontier in Europe has been often discussed, and the conflict of argument has not yet died away. It is true that in later years this country has had forced on it the task of securing colonial possessions which, in some cases for thousands of miles, march with territories held by independent, and possibly hostile States. There is, however, no comparison between an enormous territory, such as the Dominion of Canada, inhabited by an increasing and loyal population, and a fortified post, such as that of Dunkirk, the inhabitants of which were alien in race and religion from the English garrison which was to hold them down, especially as Dunkirk was a mere port on the edge of a Continent held by great nations, two of which coveted its possession, and would certainly leave no stone unturned to recover it. The only parallels in our history worth considering are the occupation of Calais in the middle ages, and of Gibraltar in modern times. It is idle to speculate whether, if Dunkirk had not been surrendered amicably to France by Charles II, it would have undergone the fate of Calais, but it is not idle to remind ourselves that, whilst Gibraltar is occupied in order to keep the sea open, and has never been used as a threat to the independence of Spain, Dunkirk, as we know from Thurloe, to whom all the secrets of Oliver's mind were revealed, was occupied in the first place, as a menace to the Dutch maritime power, and in the second place, to enable England to interfere with effect against either France or Spain, whilst it was believed by Mazarin that Oliver's main object was to crush the growing power of France. These pretensions might be condemned or defended on abstract grounds, leaving out of account any particular circumstances or any particular time. What is absolutely certain is that such a policy, if it were to be successful, required not merely the prolongation of Oliver's life, but the continuation, and more than the continuation of his military system. At a time when the English nation—it matters not whether with just cause, or from mere impatience of a taxation which it was well able to bear—was bitterly complaining of the heavy burdens imposed by the necessity of keeping up the existing army, Oliver was embarking on a foreign policy which would topple down with a crash unless that army were doubled—perhaps even trebled—to make head against the enemies it would arouse. It was a policy condemned in advance if only by the desperate financial embarrassments which must follow in its train, when France was no longer bound to England by her need of help against Spain. The hostility of France might indeed be confronted by a Government strong in the devotion of its people, and in the accumulated wealth of another half-century of commerce—strong too in an alliance with military Powers, based on the need of joining in resistance to a common danger. If Oliver had been granted those twenty more years of life which enthusiastic worshippers hold necessary for the success of his schemes, it can hardly be doubted that a European coalition would have been formed against the Protector long before it was formed against Louis XIV.

Such a danger, great as it was from the mere political claims of the Protector, was immensely increased by his attempt to inspire his foreign policy—hazardous enough in itself—with a moral and religious sentiment which found but little echo in England, and none whatever on the Continent. No doubt it was Oliver's highest glory that he aimed at something more satisfying than the material gain and the material power which are often held to be the sufficing objects of a nation's endeavour, and his interference on behalf of the victims of Piedmontese cruelty has sunk as deeply into the memories of Englishmen as the massacre of Drogheda has sunk into the memories of Irishmen. It is to be hoped that no one whose opinion is worth having will ever reproach Oliver for having sought to use his strength in defence not only of the power and interests of his country, but also of her honour—an honour which consists, not in a touchy resentment of slights, but mainly in her readiness to help in the higher service of mankind beyond her own borders as well as within them. Yet there is no effort requiring greater discretion, greater accuracy in ascertaining the relative importance of complex facts, greater knowledge of the temper of those who are likely to be affected by the action intended for the benefit of others.

It was precisely in this direction that Oliver's mind was most defective. From the beginning of the Protectorate he had overestimated the danger to Protestantism from the Roman Catholic Powers, and had striven in vain to form a great Protestant alliance to resist what was scarcely more than an imaginary danger. The massacre of the Vaudois had confirmed his belief that the danger was a permanent one, and his war with Spain had brought him into sharp antagonism with a Roman Catholic Power of intensest bigotry. We may therefore give full credence to Thurloe when he adds to the causes which induced Oliver to occupy Dunkirk, his hope that the possession of the place would be serviceable to his great design of weakening not merely Spain, but the whole House of Austria, as being engaged in a conspiracy for the injury and, if possible, the destruction of Protestantism. That this view of the case was a gross anachronism, no one familiar with the history of Europe will now deny. Isolated instances indeed there were—and there were likely to be more—of the persecution of Protestants by Roman Catholic Governments, but the tendency to form European alliances on the basis of religion was a thing of the past. So far indeed as Dunkirk was in question—and both critics and admirers of the foreign policy of the Protectorate have been apt to argue as if it concerned France and Spain alone—Oliver's intentions in this direction are of little interest, as he did not live long enough even to attempt to make his new port the basis of a European war. It is in his Baltic policy that the defects of his method were most clearly revealed.

The policy of Sweden had long been directed to the acquisition of possessions on the opposite coast of the Baltic, a policy which Oliver had more recently followed on a smaller scale with regard to the lands beyond the Channel. With a territory more thinly populated and poorer than that of England, the Kings of Sweden had, like the Commonwealth and Protectorate, gathered an army too large to be supported except by offensive war. The command of the Baltic Sea was the object in view, and in 1648, at the end of the Thirty Years' War, Sweden found herself in possession, not merely of Finland and the coast districts as far south as Riga, but of Western Pomerania, of the port of Wismar and of the secularised Bishoprics of Bremen and Verden. It was a policy even more provocative than that pursued by Oliver, because it concerned not merely the possession of a solitary point beyound the sea, but the possession of territories commanding the mouths of such rivers as the Oder, flowing into the Baltic, and the Elbe and the Weser, flowing into the North Sea. In 1655 the warrior-king, Charles X, who in the year before had succeeded to the Swedish throne upon the abdication of Christina, plunged into a war with Poland, which threatened to give him the command of the Vistula as well. In all this England had an interest because it was of great importance to her that the whole trade of the Baltic, whence she derived the materials without which she would have been unable to send her fleets to sea, should not pass entirely into the hands of one great military Power. It was this view of the case which commanded itself to the Dutch, and led in 1656 to their sending a fleet into the Baltic to preserve the independence of Dantzic. Such a view could not be lost sight of by Oliver, but it was not in his nature to content himself with the chase after purely material interests. Ever since the summer of 1655, when Charles X made overtures for his alliance, the Protector had been striving to give to it the character of a general Protestant League for the purpose of striking a blow at the German branch of the House of Austria.

Oliver's whole scheme can only be described as the product of consummate ignorance—ignorance in supposing that Charles X, aggressive, self-centred and careless of everything but his own interests as a king and as a soldier, was another Gustavus Adolphus—or rather another such disinterested enthusiast as Gustavus Adolphus appeared in the imagination of Englishmen—ignorance too in fancying that either Austria and Poland on the one hand, or Brandenburg and Denmark on the other, were likely to govern their movements by religious rather than by political motives.

The crisis came in 1657, the year in which Oliver was raised by Parliament to the constitutional Protectorate. Charles X having secured a hold on the mouth of the Vistula by his occupation of Western Prussia had naturally become an object of suspicion to Frederick William of Brandenburg—the Great Elector, as he was subsequently styled—who saw with displeasure the growing power of Sweden on the Baltic coast and who was urged by every consideration of policy to secure for himself the strip of land which intervened between part of his own possessions and the sea. Frederick III of Denmark again, fearing the ultimate loss of his own territory beyond the Sound, took the opportunity of declaring against Charles, and both Brandenburg and Denmark, Protestant as they were, looked for the support of Leopold, who had just succeeded to the Austrian hereditary estates. Leopold, however, instead of hurrying to the assistance of these two States, was held back by purely political interests, and showed little inclination to assist them. Charles X took the opportunity and led his army through Holstein into Schleswig and Jutland without difficulty, thus gaining possession of the whole of the Continental States of the King of Denmark.

The Swedish King had been ready to fool Oliver to the top of his bent. Though he had nothing of the spirit of the crusader, he was quite prepared to gain what advantage he could out of Oliver's enthusiasm. Happily for England, he had rejected the Protector's proposal—made in the spring of 1657—to take over the secularised Archbishopric of Bremen as a security for a loan, the Archbishopric being required by Oliver as a basis for an advance into Germany in an attack upon the German Catholic States, a project far more unwise than the occupation of the Flemish ports, and one which, if it had been carried into effect, would have left little room for Oliver's panegyrists to dwell upon the excellence of his foreign policy. For the remainder of the year Charles was quite ready to discuss the Protestant alliance, if only he were not required to carry it into immediate action. No doubt he would be ready to some future time to attack Austria or any other country if there was anything to be gained by it. For the present he was occupied with his quarrel with Denmark, and till that had been brought to a conclusion, there was nothing else to be done.

It was at this moment that Oliver opened the second session of his second Parliament. Full of satisfaction with his own foreign policy, he was also full of grieved surprise at the misconduct of Frederick of Denmark and of Frederick William of Brandenburg, who, not without the good will of the Dutch Republic, had thrown themselves in the path of the new Gustavus Adolphus. Within a few days of the opening of the session, Oliver held up to Parliament a picture of Papal Europe seeking "everywhere Protestants to devour." "What is there in all the parts of Europe," he asked at last, "but a consent, a co-operating, at this very time and season, to suppress everything that stands in the way of the Popish powers?" "I have," he added, "I thank God, considered, and I would beg you to consider a little with me, what that resistance is that is likely to be made to this mighty current which seems to be coming from all parts upon all Protestants? Who is there that holdeth up his head to oppose this danger? A poor prince; indeed poor; but a man in his person as gallant, and truly I think I may say, as good as any these last ages have brought forth; and a man that hath adventured his all against the Popish interest in Poland, and made his acquisition still good for the Protestant religion. He is now reduced into a corner; and what addeth to the grief of all—more grievous than all that hath been spoken of before—I wish it may not be too truly said—is, that men of our religion forget this and seek his ruin." The cause of Charles X had become very dear to Oliver, and ought, he imagined, to be very dear to the English people. The "Popish plot" against the Swedish king loomed largely in his eyes. "It is a design," he continued, "against your very being; this artifice, and this complex design against the Protestant interest—wherein so many Protestants are not so right as were to be wished! If they can shut us out of the Baltic Sea,"—with Oliver the consideration of material prosperity was never far distant from his spiritual enthusiams—"and make themselves masters of that, where is your trade? Where are your materials to preserve your shipping? Where will you be able to challenge any right by sea, or justify yourselves against a foreign invasion on your own soil? Think upon it; this is the design! I believe if you will go and ask the poor mariner in his red cap and coat, as he passeth from ship to ship, you will hardly find in any ship but they will tell you this is designed against you. So obvious is it, by this and other things, that you are the object; and, in my conscience, I know not for what else, but because of the purity of the profession amongst you, who have not yet made it your trade to prefer your profit before your godliness, but reckon godliness the greater gain."

It was Oliver's head—not his heart—that was at fault. But a few days after these words were spoken, Charles X was tramping with his army over the ice of the two Belts, in that marvellous march which landed him in Zealand, and compelled Frederick III to sign the Treaty of Roeskilde which abandoned to Sweden the Danish possessions to the east of the Sound. What then were Oliver's Ambassadors doing when that treaty was negotiating? They were but arguing as any Dutchman or Brandenburger might have argued, on behalf of the material interests of their own country. They favoured Charles's wish to annex the Danish provinces beyond the Sound, because it would leave the passage into the Baltic under the control of two Powers instead of one. They opposed his wish to annex more than two provinces of Norway, in order that the monopoly of the timber trade might not fall into his hands. Of the Protestant alliance not a word was spoken.

For all that, the Protestant alliance had not passed out of Oliver's mind. Now that Denmark was crushed, Charles professed himself to be quite ready to attack Leopold of Austria, if only he were allowed to crush Brandenburg first; and in May an English Ambassador was sent to Berlin to plead with the Elector of Brandenburg to join England and Sweden against Leopold, to whose support Frederick William was looking against an unprovoked attack from Charles. Happily for England, Frederick William refused to countenance this insane proposal, and in August Charles renewed the war against Denmark, with a fixed determination to bring the whole of the Scandinavian territory under his own sway, before he involved himself in those further complications in Germany, in which Oliver, supported by Mazarin, was anxious to involve him. "France," said the King of Sweden, "wants to limit me and to prescribe the course I am to take, and England attempts to do the same, but I will put myself in a position to be independent of their orders." His Ministers spoke even more openly of their future plans. When Denmark and Norway had been annexed, and the Baltic brought under the undisputed control of Sweden, Courland and West Prussia must inevitably pass into their master's hands. Then with an army of 40,000 men, supported by a navy of 100 ships, the Swedish army would march through Germany into Italy, visit the Pope, and plunder Rome. "Their first thought is pillage," added the French Ambassador who reported these vapourings perhaps not without exaggeration. Charles X was a great soldier, but he was by no means the oppressed saint of Oliver's imagination.

There can be little doubt that the maintenance of a war in the heart of Germany, even with a Swedish ally, would have been far beyond Oliver's means. The occupation of the Flemish ports had taxed his resources to the uttermost. In the speech in which he had sung the high praises of the

Swedish king, he had been obliged to plead the necessities of the army as a ground for his demand for fresh supplies. The pay of the army was far in arrear, and it was on the army that he depended to keep down hostile parties at home and to stave off a Royalist attack from abroad. Nor was that army needed for purposes of mere defence. Picturing to himself the majority of the Continental nations as actuated by a wild desire to assail England, he inferred that attack was the best defence. "You have counted yourselves happy," he said to Parliament, "in being environed with a great ditch from all the world beside. Truly you will not be able to keep your ditch, nor your shipping, unless you turn your ships and shipping into troops of horse and companies of foot; and fight to defend yourselves on *terra firma*."

This then was what Oliver's much-lauded foreign policy had come to—more regiments, and even higher taxation than what the vast majority of Englishmen believed to be far too high already. A great Continental war, with all its risks and burdens, was dangled before the eyes of a Parliament to which such an outlook had no attractions. That Parliament was no longer the body which had voted the new constitution. Not only were there now two Houses, but the composition of the older House had been significantly altered. The most determined supporters of the Protectorate had been withdrawn to occupy the benches of the new House, whilst the clause of *The Humble Petition and Advice,* which prohibited the Protector from ever again excluding members duly elected from what had now become the House of Commons, opened its doors to his most determined enemies. The men who now found their way to their seats, such as Hazlerigg and Scot, were opposed heart and soul to the whole system of the Protectorate, and longed for the re-establishment of Parliamentry supremacy. Such men were the more dangerous because they were sufficiently versed in Parliamentary tactics to know the advantage of a rallying cry which would bring the lukewarm to their side. The powers and attributes of the other House were ill-defined in the constitutional document to which it owed its birth, and it was easy to gain adherents by urging that it was not entitled to the name or the privileges of the House of Lords of the Monarchy. After some days of wrangling, the Protector resolved to put an end to the debates. It was hard, he complained, to have accepted a constitutional settlement on the invitation of that very Parliament, and then to have it brought into question. "I can say," he continued, "in the presence of God—in comparison with whom we are but like poor creeping ants upon the earth—I would have been glad to have lived under my wood side to have kept a flock of sheep, rather than to have undertaken such a government as this. But undertaking it by the advice and petition of you, I did look that you who had offered it unto me should make it good."

Such language must appear to those who judge by the recorded words and actions of this Parliament to be without adequate justification. It is undeniable that the constitution contained no definition of the powers of the new House, and if there had been no other than the ostensible question at issue, it would have been unreasonable in Oliver to hurry on a crisis before attempting, directly or indirectly, to suggest terms of compromise. As a matter of fact this question of the other House was very far from covering the whole ground of debate. A petition to which thousands of signatures were appended was being circulated in the City, asking for a complete restitution of Parliamentary supremacy and—no doubt to catch the support of a certain section of the army—for an enactment that no officer or soldier should be cashiered without the sentence of a court martial. Oliver was perfectly right in holding that the attack on the other House was equivalent to an assault on the constitutional Protectorate. He had himself looked to that House as restoring to him in another form the powers which he had abandoned when he let fall the Instrument. By keeping in his own hands the selection of its members, and providing that that House should have a veto on subsequent nominations—the principle of inheritance being totally excluded—he imagined that he had sufficiently provided for the future. His objects in so doing may be taken as those set forth by a writer who had ample means of gathering his intentions. "It was no small task for the Protector to find idoneous men for this place, because the future security of the honest interest seemed—under God —to be laid up in them; for by a moral generation, if they were well chosen at the first, they would propagate their own kind, when the single person could not, and the Commons, who represented the nation, would not, having in them for the most part the spirit of those they represent, which hath little affinity with a respect of the cause of God." It is easy to criticise such a principle from a modern point of view. Yet if the morality of Oliver's political actions are ever to be judged fairly, it must never be forgotten that the right of an honest Government to prevent the people from injuring themselves by out-voting the saner members of the community was—rather than any democratic or Parliamentary theory—the predominant note of his career. It is this at least which explains his assent to the choice of the nominated Parliament, as well as his breach with the Parliaments which he dismissed in 1655 and 1658.

Such views could not but lead the Protector to a breach with his second Parliament as well. The men who were grumbling at the insolence of his new lords were, as he well knew, prepared to follow up their attack by another more directly aimed at his own authority. The remainder of the Protector's speech is only intelligible on this supposition. Professing his intention to stand by the new constitution, he accused his opponents of a design to subvert it. "These things," he asseverated, "lead to nothing else but to the playing of the King of Scots' game—if I may so call him—and I think myself bound before God to do what I can to prevent it; and if this be so, I do assign it to this cause—your not assenting to what you did invite me to by your Petition and Advice, as that which might prove the settlement of the nation; and if this be the end of your sitting, and this be your carriage, I think it high time that an end be put to your sitting. And I do dissolve this Parliament! And let God be judge between you and me!"

No man knew better than Oliver the weight of the blow that had fallen on him. His attempt to govern constitutionally with a Parliamentary constitution had proved as impracticable as his attempt to govern constitutionally with a military constitution. For a whole week he shut himself up, meditating apart from his Council on the means of repairing the disaster. Only once during the whole time did he even appear in his family circle. Then after prolonged consultation with advisers gathered from far and near, he resolved to summon another Parliament to meet in that very spring. He at least would stand firmly by the constitution to which he had sworn, and he could but hope that the nation would be equally loyal when the choice between ordered liberty and the unrestricted government of a single House was fairly set before the electors. It was the remedy applied afterwards by William III to a similar mischief, and not applied in vain.

Unfortunately for Cromwell the circumstances were not the same. It is unnecessary here to discuss the relative merits of written and unwritten constitutions on the one hand, or of a dominant Parliament and a dominant executive on the other. The one form of government or the other may be desirable in different nations or at different times. The one thing needful is that the institutions of a nation, whatever they be, shall be supported by the national sentiment. It was this that Oliver had never succeeded in evoking, because he had never appealed to it, and he was hardly likely to succeed in evoking it now. He could, for a time—and only for a time—rule England with an army. He could not rule it with a piece of paper. At no long distance, as he already saw, the unchecked supremacy of Parliament would bring back the Stuarts, because the traditional hold of the old monarchy upon the minds of men was the only power capable of keeping in check alike the tyranny of the army, and the anarchy which could not but arise if contending parties were left to struggle for the mastery without fear of military intervention. Oliver's own power for good was growing feebler. Financial embarrassments gathered round him. The sailors and soldiers went unpaid, even though Bremen had not been occupied and no English army was struggling—it can hardly be doubted—towards certain defeat in the heart of Germany.

The Parliament he contemplated never came into existence. Another great Royalist plot took up for a time all the energies of the Government. Oliver, with his usual clemency, contented himself with two executions, those of Dr. Hewit and Sir Henry Slingsby, whilst three more victims expiated their share in a project for raising a tumult in London. Once again affairs appeared to take a more favourable turn. The victory of the Dunes, in which the French army, aided by 6,000 English troops, overthrew the Spaniards, was won on June 4, whilst the surrender of Dunkirk on the 14th, together with the subsequent gains of the allies in Flanders put out of the question any landing of the exiled King in England with Spanish aid. The thought of bringing a new Parliament together might seem capable of realisation under these happy auspices, and preparations were made for its meeting in November.

Whether that Parliament, if ever it had met, would have supported the Protectorate more firmly than its predecessors, is a question which can never be answered. All that can be said is that the radical elements of the situation remained unchanged. Oliver had been deeply saddened by his failure, and his anxious thoughts told on his already enfeebled health. Death had been busy in his family circle. Young Rich, the newly wedded husband of his daughter Frances, died in February.* On August 6 his best-beloved daughter, Lady Claypole, passed away after a long and painful illness. Oliver's sorrowing vigils by her bedside broke down what remained to him of bodily endurance. Now and again indeed he was able to take the air, and on one of these occasions George Fox coming to talk with him on the persecutions of the Friends, marked the changed expression of his face. "Before I came to him," noted Fox, "as he rode at the head of his life-guard, I saw and felt a waft of death go forth against him; and when I came to him he looked like a dead man." On August 24 the Protector moved to Whitehall. The ague from which he suffered increased in violence. On Sunday, August 29, prayers were offered up in the churches for his recovery. The following day was the day of that great storm which fixed itself in the memory of that generation. The devil,

* Her second marriage with Sir John Russell took place after the Restoration.

said the Cavaliers, had come to fetch home the soul of the murderer and tyrant. Around the bedside of the dying potentate more friendly eyes were keeping watch. "The doctors," wrote Thurloe to Henry Cromwell far away in Ireland, "are yet hopeful that he may struggle through it, though their hopes are mingled with much fear." Twenty-four hours later the hopeful signs were still dwelt on. "The Lord," wrote Fleetwood, "is pleased to give some little reviving this evening; after a few slumbering sleeps, his pulse is better." Scriptural words of warning and comfort were constantly on the sick man's lips. "It is a fearful thing," he three times repeated, "to fall into the hands of the living God." The anxious questioning was answered by his strong assurance of mercy. "Lord," he muttered, as the evening drew in, "though I am a miserable and wretched creature, I am in Covenant with Thee through grace, and I may, I will come to Thee for Thy people. Thou hast made made me, though very unworthy, a mean instrument to do them some good, and Thee service, and many of them have set too high a value upon me, though others wish, and would be glad of my death. Lord, however Thou do dispose of me, continue and go on to do good for them. Give them consistency of judgment, one heart, and mutual love; and go on to deliver them, and with the work of reformation, and make the name of Christ glorious in the world. Teach those who look too much on Thy instruments to depend more upon Thyself. Pardon such as desire to trample upon the dust of a poor worm, for they are Thy people too. And pardon the folly of this short prayer; even for Jesus Christ's sake. And give us a good night, if it be Thy pleasure. Amen."

Before long hope ceased to be possible. Oliver himself knew that his life was rapidly drawing to an end. "I would," he said, "be willing to be further serviceable to God and His people, but my work is done." A few more prayers, a few more words, and on September 3, the anniversary of Dunbar and Worcester, as well as of the hopeful meeting of his first Parliament, the tried servant of God and of his country entered into the appointed rest from all his labours.

The man—it is ever so with the noblest—was greater than

his work. In his own heart lay the resolution to subordinate self to public ends, and to subordinate material to moral and spiritual objects of desire. His work was accomplished under the conditions to which all human effort is subject. He was limited by the defects which make imperfect the character and intellect even of the noblest and the wisest of mankind. He was limited still more by the unwillingness of his contemporaries to mould themselves after his ideas. The blows that he had struck against the older system had their enduring effects. Few wished for the revival of the absolute kingship, of the absolute authority of a single House of Parliament, or of the Laudian system of governing the Church. In the early part of his career Oliver was able to say with truth of his own position: "No one rises so high as he who knows not whither he is going." The living forces of England—forces making for the destruction of those barriers which he was himself breaking through, buoyed him up—as a strong and self-confident swimmer, he was carried onward by the flowing tide. In the latter portion of the Protector's career it was far otherwise. His failure to establish a permanent Government was not due merely to his deficiency in constructive imagination. It was due rather to two causes: the umbrage taken at his position as head of an army whose interference in political affairs gave even more offence than the financial burdens it imposed on a people unaccustomed to regular taxation; and the reaction which set in against the spiritual claims of that Puritanism of which he had become the mouth-piece. The first cause of offence requires no further comment. As for the second, it is necessary to lay aside all sectarian preoccupations, if ever a true historic judgment is to be formed. It was no reaction against the religious doctrines or ecclesiastical institutions upheld by the Protector that brought about the destruction of his system of government. It is in the highest degree unlikely that a revolution would ever have taken place merely to restore episcopacy or the Book of Common Prayer. So far as the reaction was not directed against militarism, it was directed against the introduction into the political world of what appeared to be too high a standard of morality, a reaction which struck specially upon Puritanism, but which would have struck with as much force upon any other form of religion which, like that upheld by Laud, called in the power of the State to enforce its claims.

Nor is this all that can be said. Even though Oliver was in his own person no sour fanatic, as Royalist pamphleteers after the Restoration falsely asserted; it is impossible to deny that he strove by acts of government to lead men into the paths of morality and religion beyond the limit which average human nature had fixed for itself. In dealing with foreign nations his mistake on this head was more conspicuous, because he had far less knowledge of the conditions of efficient action abroad than he had at home. It may fairly be said that he knew less of Scotland than of England, less of Ireland than of Great Britain, and less of the Continent than of any one of the three nations over which he ruled. It has sometimes been said that Oliver made England respected in Europe. It would be more in accordance with truth to say that he made her feared.

It is unnecessary here to pursue this subject further. The development of this theme is for the historian of England rather than for the biographer of the Protector. Oliver's claim to greatness can be tested by the undoubted fact that his character receives higher and wider appreciation as the centuries pass by. The limitations on his nature—the one-sidedness of his religious zeal, the mistakes of his policy—are thrust out of sight, the nobility of his motives, the strength of his character, and the breadth of his intellect, force themselves on the minds of generations for which the objects for which he strove have been for the most part attained, though often in a different fashion from that which he placed before himself. Even those who refuse to waste a thought on his spiritual aims remember with gratitude his constancy of effort to make England great by land and sea; and it would be well for them also to be reminded of his no less constant efforts to make England worthy of greatness.

Of the man himself, it is enough to repeat the words of one who knew him well: "His body was well compact and strong; his stature under six feet—I believe about two inches —his head so shaped as you might see it a store-house and shop both—of a vast treasury of natural parts. His temper exceeding fiery, as I have known; but the flame of it kept down for the most part, or soon allayed with those moral endowments he had. He was naturally compassionate towards objects in distress, even to an effeminate measure; though God had made him a heart wherein was left little room for any fear but was due to Himself, of which there was a large proportion—yet did he exceed in tenderness towards sufferers. A larger soul, I think, hath seldom dwelt in a house of clay."